Why So Stupid?

How the Human Race has
Never Really Learned to Think

About the Author

Edward de Bono was born in the island of Malta, which may have the oldest civilization in the world. The oldest man-made structure in the world is a stone age temple in Gozo, the sister island to Malta. He qualified as a medical doctor (M.D.) at the University of Malta and then proceeded as a Rhodes Scholar to Christ Church, Oxford, where he studied Psychology and Physiology (M.A.). He returned to medicine and obtained a D.Phil. at Oxford for his research on the system control of blood pressure. He had a faculty appointment at Oxford and then moved to the University of London at St. Thomas Hospital where he continued his work on biological system behaviour. He then moved to Cambridge University and helped set up the Department of Investigative Medicine. He was granted a Ph.D. from Cambridge. The next move was to the medical faculty at Harvard University. After Harvard he returned to Cambridge and eventually took early retirement to continue with his work in 'thinking'.

From psychology came an interest in thinking. From medicine came an understanding of biological system behaviour. When this system behaviour was applied to the neural networks in the brain there was formed the basis for the design of new thinking tools. Creativity was no longer a mystery but the behaviour of information in self-organising systems that form asymmetric patterns. From this came the design of the deliberate creative processes of 'lateral thinking' (provocation, random entry, etc.). From an appreciation of the huge importance of perception came the deliberate attention-directing tools of the CoRT programme. 'Parallel thinking' came later, following an appreciation of the primitive nature of argument. All these methods have been used successfully over many years both in business and in schools.

Edward de Bono has been called 'the father of thinking about thinking'. He has written 67 books with translations into 37 languages. His methods are taught in thousands of schools around the world and are mandatory on the curriculum in many countries. His instruction in thinking has been sought by many business organizations over the years, including: IBM, Prudential, Shell, Exxon, NTT, Nokia, Bank of America, Union Bank of Switzerland, GM, etc. He is on the Accenture list of the fifty most influential business thinkers in the world. Unusual clients include the Australian national cricket team. He is listed as one of twenty living visionaries by a leading Austrian business journal.

The International Astronomical Union named a minor planet after him: DE73 became edebono. A group of academics in South Africa nominated him as one of the 250 people who had most contributed in the whole history of humanity. The University of Pretoria and the University of Malta have both set up 'de Bono Institutes'. The University of Pretoria has also made him the first 'Professor of Thinking' in the world. The Royal Melbourne Institute of Technology recently awarded him the degree of Doctor of Design. There is a 'de Bono Institute' in Melbourne set up and endowed by Ron Andrews. In 2005 he was appointed Da Vinci Professor of Thinking at the University of Advancing Technology, Arizona, and Professor of Constructive Thinking at Dublin City University. He was awarded LLD by University of Dundee.

Peter Ueberroth attributed part of his great success in organizing the 1984 Los Angeles Olympic Games to his use of de Bono's lateral thinking methods which he had learned some years earlier at a YPO (Young Presidents Organisation) meeting in Florida.

Edward de Bono is the inventor of what may be the world's simplest real game: the L-Game.

Why So Stupid?

How the Human Race has Never Really Learned to Think

Edward de Bono

BP
BLACKHALL
PUBLISHING

This book was typeset by Susan Waine for

BLACKHALL PUBLISHING
33 Carysfort Avenue
Blackrock
Co. Dublin
Ireland

e-mail: info@blackhallpublishing.com
www.blackhallpublishing.com

ISBN: 1 842180 98 3 PB
ISBN: 1 842180 50 9 HB

A catalogue record for this book is
available from the British Library.

Printed by Athenaeum Press Ltd

Contents

Readers should compile their own Contents page, including areas that are of most relevance or interest to them.

Foreword

Do you think about thinking? Probably not. Most people do not think about thinking. You walk, you eat, you sleep, you cough, you think. These things do not need thinking about. You decide what you want to do and then search your memory for the usual way of doing it. That is all there is to thinking.

And yet, nothing is more important than human thinking. The quality of your personal future depends on your thinking. The quality of the future of the human race depends on thinking. What else could it depend upon?

Maybe we have neglected thinking. Maybe we have taken it for granted. Maybe we have believed, and still believe, that there is nothing more that can be done about thinking. We have an excellent 'thinking system' and nothing more needs to be done.

That is where I disagree. We do have an excellent thinking system – but it is inadequate. Our thinking system is all directed at the past. We recognize standard situations and provide standard answers. We have never developed the creative thinking needed to design the way forward. Our thinking is excellent for technology and almost useless in human affairs.

Descartes (the famous French philosopher)
'*Cogito ergo sum.*'
'I think therefore I am.'

De Bono (the infamous Maltese thinker)
'*Ago ergo erigo.*'
'I act therefore I construct.'

Thinking is not just about philosophical reflections and analysis. Thinking is about getting things done, making things happen and making progress.

We have so neglected 'thinking' as an operating skill that there was not, as far as I know, a single university in the world which actually had a 'Professor of thinking'. That was the case when this book was written. Since then, I have been made professor of thinking at the University of

Pretoria – the largest university in Africa. In 2005 I was appointed Da Vinci Professor of Thinking at the University of Advancing Technology, Arizona, and Professor of Constructive Thinking at Dublin City University.

Rodin did a great disservice to thinking with his sculpture of 'the thinker'. The impression is one of solemnity, seriousness and grim hard work. But thinking can be fun and lively. Four year olds in school can enjoy thinking as much as philosophers and rocket scientists.

There is but one attitude with which this book should be read:

'Just suppose he is right?'

The implications are huge. Some new methods are suggested in the book. Years of experience with these methods show that they work and are greatly superior to some existing thinking habits. That is not important. Such methods are only a beginning. There is very much more to be done.

The big change is that for the first time in history we can design thinking methods based on how the brain actually works – instead of playing with the word games of philosophy.

'Schools waste two thirds of the talent in society and universities sterilize the other third.'

'The apparent purpose of education is to convince two thirds of the students that they really are stupid.'

Youngsters who do not do well at the 'school game' leave school thinking they are stupid. Yet they are not stupid at all. They can be very good 'thinkers' if given the chance. Five hours of thinking given to unemployed youngsters increased the employment rate five fold.

Universities are obsessed with history, scholarship and analysis. These do have their value and their place. But there should be equal emphasis on constructive thinking, on creative thinking and on design thinking. Knowledge is not enough. Value creation needs a different sort of thinking.

So I invite you to read this book not in a defensive, adversarial or critical frame of mind but in an effort to get something from it. Around the world there are thousands of executives and thousands of school children who have already found that thinking can be made much more powerful.

It is time we paid serious attention to 'thinking'. Complacency with our existing thinking habits is not only limiting but has become very, very dangerous.

EDWARD DE BONO

Acknowledgements

This book is dedicated to
Daniela, Francesca, Joan, Helene, Tatiana, Sandra, Marisa, Debbie, Pam,
Diane, Marysia and Svetlana, all of whom provided the environment
in which the book was written.

You can analyze the past but you have to design the future.

The Renaissance was the greatest intellectual disaster in Western civilization.

The excellence of the thinking system provided by the Renaissance has prevented us from seeing the inadequacy of that system.

This is a quiet book about a rather important subject.

Nothing is more fundamental than human thinking.

Nothing is more important than human thinking.

The quality of our future will depend directly on the excellence of our thinking.

A cook uses a variety of ingredients and the capabilities of the available stove.

Beliefs, values, ethics, morals, principles and information are ingredients that are put together by human thinking. History is full of examples of what happens when an ingredient is substituted for thinking.

It is unfortunate, but perhaps unavoidable, that those most likely to be upset by this book will be those who most need the book.

Perhaps that perceived need is the basis of the resistance.

For the first time in human history we can relate thinking directly to the behaviour of the brain.

We no longer have to be content with games played with words.

From an understanding of the system basis of the brain we can design new thinking methods that take us beyond descriptions of what seems to happen.

Humour is by far the most significant behaviour of the human brain.

Humour tells us more about how the brain works than any other human activity.

Reason tells us very little because any sorting system run backwards is a reasoning system.

We see the great success of human thinking in some areas.

In other areas we see a considerable failure of human thinking.

Why should that be?

When my friend Buzz Aldrin, the astronaut, walked on the surface of the moon, that was a great triumph of human thinking.

When I pick up my mobile phone in London to call my friend Sophie in Melbourne on her mobile phone, that is a great triumph of human thinking.

The elimination of the disease of smallpox from the world is a great triumph of human thinking. At one time smallpox was a deadly disease that killed hundreds of thousands of people.

When you fly across the Atlantic in the Concorde at a speed faster than the speed of sound, that is a great triumph of human thinking.

Through the power of television, and courtesy of CNN, an event taking place somewhere in the world can be watched at the same time by millions across the world. That is a triumph of human thinking.

Unlocking the energy of the atom itself is a great triumph of human thinking. The use of this energy may be for peaceful purposes or for destruction.

Mapping out the human genome is a triumph of human thinking. From this arises the possibility of treatment for genetic diseases.

It would be difficult to give a complete list of the great successes of human thinking in science and technology.

Why has human thinking been so successful in science and technology yet so unsuccessful in human affairs?

The answer to this question arises directly from the thinking system and habits introduced at the Renaissance.

The conflict in the Middle East illustrates better than anything else the failure of human thinking when applied to human affairs.

Two of the most intelligent groups on the surface of the planet know they are going to have to live together, but seem unable to design a way of doing so.

The important word is 'design'.

When a scientist has before him the element of iron, the scientist knows the properties of iron: can be magnetized, conducts electricity, oxidizes, etc. These will always be the properties of iron. You can predict these properties with certainty. You can make use of these properties to design pieces of technology.

It is this permanence and predictability which enables science and technology to move ahead so rapidly.

In human affairs it is different. If you call someone an 'idiot', then that person is no longer the same person you called an idiot. The person has changed as a result of being called an idiot by you. In human affairs there are complex interactive loops. Our traditional thinking habits with their judgement base assume a permanence and predictability that do not exist in human affairs.

Is it really possible to change human thinking in a way that is significant, practical, effective and simple?

The answer is 'Yes'.

In a platinum mine in South Africa there were seven different tribes working alongside each other. There were around two hundred and ten fights and disputes every month. Susan Mackie and her coll-eague Donalda Dawson taught new thinking methods to these miners, most of whom had never been to school even for one day. The number of fights dropped from two hundred and ten to just four. Productivity in the mine rose considerably. Human nature had not changed, nor had historical hatreds between the tribes. But behaviour had changed dramatically. What was taught directly to these miners was not traditional thinking but new, and very simple, thinking methods.

A major Scandinavian corporation used to spend thirty days on their multi-national project discussions. Using the new method of 'parallel thinking' they completed their discussions in just two days.

MDS, a Canadian corporation that makes medical equipment, did a careful costing and showed that in the first year 'parallel thinking' was used they saved more than twenty million dollars.

In the United Kingdom the government has a special programme for unemployed youngsters called 'The New Deal'. The Holst Group taught some of the new thinking methods to some of these unemployed youngsters for just five hours in all. The employment rate increased five-fold. A year later ninety per cent of the youngsters were still off the unemployment register.

In Australia, Jennifer O'Sullivan taught these new methods to unemployed youngsters in Job Clubs (a government programme). The usual rate of employment from such clubs was forty per cent. She got one hundred per cent employment in one club and seventy per cent in another. Every one of the youngsters was completely deaf.

The Hungerford Guidance Centre in London takes youngsters who are too violent to be taught in normal schools. When David Lane was running the centre he started teaching the new thinking methods. He reported that the level of 'serious incidents' dropped from the usual eight a week to just one. David Lane has now done a twenty year follow up and has shown that the rate of actual criminal conviction for those taught 'thinking' is less than one tenth of the rate for those not taught thinking. This is a very powerful effect.

I once taught a class of twelve-year-old boys in a school in Sydney, Australia. I asked them what they thought of the idea of every student being paid ten dollars a week just for going to school. All thirty of the youngsters liked the idea. I then asked them to use one of the simple attention-directing tools (from the CoRT – Cognitive Research Trust – programme). As a result of thinking more broadly, twenty-nine out of the thirty had changed their minds and decided it was not a good idea at all.

Grant Todd in the USA has been working to introduce 'parallel thinking' to jury deliberations. In one complex case in Wisconsin, with thirty-two questions for the jury, use of the method gave a unanimous result in a short time. These trials wih juries have been so successful that the law has been amended to allow judges to ask that the jury 'be trained in thinking'. This is a huge change in the jury system.

I was once told by someone from a senior IBM laboratory that the use of parallel thinking had reduced meeting times to one quarter of what they had been.

Kathy Myers, who runs the APTT training from Iowa, has many other stories to tell of the business use of new thinking methods.

Carol Ferguson set up one hundred and thirty workshops one afternoon for a steel company. Using just one of the deliberate creative tools of lateral thinking they generated twenty-one thousand ideas that afternoon. It took nine months to sort through the ideas.

I once had a class of eleven Nobel Prize laureates to whom I taught some of these thinking methods. At the end of three days they agreed that the methods worked and three of them then wrote forewords to my book *I am Right, You are Wrong* (Penguin 1991).

On another occasion I taught thinking to a group of severe Down's Syndrome youngsters. Given some simple thinking tools their thinking was very good indeed.

The largest direct class I have ever had was one of seven thousand four hundred youngsters (aged six to twelve years old) in Christchurch, New Zealand, organized by Vicki Buck, the mayoress of that city.

Peter and Linda Low in Singapore have been very successful in teaching these new methods to business, to government and to education. They also run a special Saturday School for teaching thinking. I have visited this school and it is clear that the youngsters love thinking. After the Tsunami in Sri Lanka the various aid agencies could not agree on the way forward. After two weeks of disagreement the government asked Peter Low to introduce de Bono parallel thinking. In two days they had a blue print of the way forward. The government now insists that the aid agencies learn the thinking metods.

A school principal once told me that youngsters loved the 'thinking class' so much that a major form of punishment was to forbid those who misbehaved from attending these classes (for a while).

There are also several examples (from the Holst Group and from John Edwards) of how the direct teaching of thinking in schools improved academic and exam performance to a marked extent.

Denis Inwood of the Atkey organisation has done research showing that the explicit teaching of thinking as a skill increased performance in every subject by between thirty and one hundred per cent.

The really sad thing is that so few people in education know that thinking is not just a matter of intelligence, but can be taught directly as a skill.

So few people know that new thinking methods exist and have been used successfully for many years. Most government advisors are rather out of date on these matters.

If the human race has not been thinking, then what has it been doing?

The answer is 'recognition'.

The Greek Gang of Three gave us a thinking system based on recognition.

A child is brought to a doctor in a clinic. The child has a rash. The doctor examines the child, listens to the history of the illness and perhaps does some tests (to exclude possibilities).

The doctor then makes a diagnosis of 'measles'.
Once the diagnosis is made then the doctor knows the likely course of the illness. The doctor knows the possible complications to look out for – such as ear infections. The doctor can now prescribe the necessary treatment and care. The doctor also arranges to keep an eye on the patient.

So the first step is collecting the information (tests, history, examin-ation, etc.). The second step is to list some 'possibilities'. The third step is to seek to eliminate the possibilities – leaving the doctor with the possibility that cannot be eliminated. This is the diagnosis.

What is the doctor really doing?

The doctor is seeking to recognize a 'standard situation' which has been encountered over and again by others and given the name 'measles'.

The diagnosis of measles gives the communication channel between the total experience of the medical profession and the need for action in this particular case.

When the head of the Federal Reserve Bank in Washington, looks at the economy, he is seeking standard situations. If there seems to be inflation, then the standard response is to raise interest rates. If there seems to be a recession then the standard response is to lower interest rates. When there is not a clear standard situation, then things become more difficult – and you have to look for 'non-standard' but recognizable situations or combinations of situations.

We do this all the time. This 'recognition' is the basis of all our thinking.

If the situation is complex we may need to analyze the situation in order to identify the standard components. Almost all the thinking done in universities is concerned with just such analyses. If you do not understand or know how to deal with a complex situation then you seek to break it down into known parts, elements or forces.

The system works very well indeed and is very powerful. It is seen at its best in science and technology.

The Renaissance re-introduced into Europe, and Western civilization, the thinking of the Greek Gang of Three.

This then became the standard 'software' of

Western thinking and has remained so to this day.

The Gang of Three was Socrates, Plato and Aristotle.

As a young man Plato knew Socrates even though Plato was not formally a student of Socrates. Socrates never wrote anything. Plato wrote up Socrates in his work (*The Dialogues*, etc.).

Aristotle was a student of Plato's and later became the tutor of Alexander the Great.
After the Roman Empire collapsed, Europe lapsed into the 'Dark Ages' and Greek and Roman thinking was largely forgotten. It is said that Charlemagne, who was the greatest leader in Europe, could not read or write.

Hellenic culture had gone to North Africa and to Alexander in particular. When the Arabs were in Spain they brought Hellenic culture with them. It was the Arab philosophers in Spain that re-introduced Greek thinking into Europe at the Renaissance.

This thinking was eagerly taken up by the Christian church under people like Thomas Aquinas of Naples. There was a need for a way of thinking that could be used to prove heretics wrong. The thinking of the Gang of Three provided just this.

As the Church largely controlled schools, universities and intellectual culture, this method of thinking quickly became the basic software of Western thinking and has remained so to this day. This is not surprising because it is, indeed, a powerful method of thinking. And there was no other thinking method around.

Socrates was very interested in dialectic or argument. His reputation is based on his method of asking questions. These were not 'searching questions' but 'checking-out questions'. For example, Socrates would ask:

'Would you choose your best athlete by chance?' Obvious answer is 'No'.

'Would you choose the best navigator for your ship by chance?' Obvious answer is 'No'.

'So does it make sense to choose our politicians by chance?' Expected answer is 'No'.

In a typical Socratic fashion, this ignores the reason behind choosing politicians by chance (at some stage in the election of the Council of Five Hundred), which was to avoid bribery, factions and corruption. These factors are very important in politics but irrelevant for athletes and navigators.

Plato was strongly influenced by Pythagoras and believed that just as there were ultimate truths in mathematics so there should be ultimate truths in everything. He was therefore concerned with the search for the 'inner truth' that lay below the surface.

Plato did not believe in democracy and thought it a rather silly system – possibly because the Athenian government was heavily taxing his family, which was one of the rich families in Athens. Plato's design for a modern state was a book called *The Republic*. There is to be no voting but the 'scientific breeding' of rulers. There are to be no families but government crèches for children. It is said that the book became standard doctrine for the Nazi party in Germany.

The Sophists were thinkers who lived largely outside Athens where the Gang of Three lived. So they were provincial thinkers, many of whom were concerned with 'word play' and tricky argument games.

Protagoras was a Sophist but a very modern system thinker. He said that if you put manure on the roots of a plant the plant thrived. But if you put the same manure on the leaves of the plant the plant would die. In the same way he said that if you gave this substance now it would cure the illness, but if you gave it later it would have no effect. If you gave twice as much of the substance you might even kill the patient. So you could not claim that something was 'good' or 'bad'. It depended on the whole 'system'. Plato and his followers suppressed the Sophists.

Aristotle believed that men had more teeth in their mouth than did women. Although he was married twice he never asked his wives to open their mouths to have their teeth counted. He did not need to count their teeth because he knew. He knew because with horses the stallion has more teeth than the mare. So Aristotle established a general principle that the male of the species has more teeth than the female. So he had to have more teeth than his wives.

Aristotle's great contribution was to set up these principles, boxes or categories. These would all be based on past experience. Just as medical experience established the 'box' of measles so experience would establish many other boxes.

All a thinker now had to do was to judge whether the encountered situation did or did not fit into a particular box. It could not be half in and half out. It was either in the box or not in the box – there was nowhere else it could be.

That is how the 'recognition' mode of thinking came about. It is very powerful and very effective and has served us well in science and technology where the 'boxes' are fixed and permanent.

I have no quarrel with this thinking method – but it is not enough.

I have nothing against the front left wheel of a motor car. But if you believed that a front left wheel was all you needed on a motor car, then I would have a problem with that belief.

Our traditional thinking (recognition based) is excellent but it is not enough.

Our traditional thinking is concerned with:

'What is'

It is not good at all at designing:

'What can be'

The difference is between 'judgement' and 'design'.

The human brain is designed to form standard patterns for dealing with a stable world.

The Gang of Three thinking emphasizes and enhances this natural behaviour of the brain.

One day a fellow got up in the morning and set his computer to figure out all the different ways of getting dressed with eleven pieces of clothing. The computer took forty hours of continuous processing to work it out.

This is hardly surprising because with eleven pieces of clothing there are 39,916,800 ways of getting dressed. The overall calculation is easy enough. There are eleven choices for the first item, ten choices for the second item, etc.

If the brain did things this way then we should need to live to the age of seventy-six, using our entire waking life trying ways of getting dressed.

You may argue that it is obvious that you cannot put your shoes on before you put your socks on. This is not obvious; it is behaviour 'learned' from past experience.

If the brain really worked like this it would be impossible to get dressed, get to the office, read, write, etc.

Of course the brain does not work like this at all. The purpose and function of the brain is to allow incoming information to form itself into patterns.

Once a pattern is formed then all you need to do is start the patterns and each step then follows without further thought.

The definition of a pattern is simple.

'If at every moment the next step has a higher probability of being taken than any other step, then you are on a pattern.' Patterns may be strong or they may be weak.

The brain is a 'self-organizing' information system. This means that incoming information organizes itself into patterns. Rain falling on a landscape gradually organizes itself into streams and rivers. Once formed these streams and rivers collect and capture all future rainfall. In the same way, the patterns formed in the brain determine our future perceptions.

There is no 'mystery' about this process. I explained the process in broad detail in my book *The Mechanism of Mind* (Simon & Schuster 1969 and Penguin UK). At least two groups have set up computer simulations and shown that the system laid out works as claimed. The leading physicist in the world, Nobel prize winner Murray Gell Mann once told me: 'You have stumbled across these things ten years before mathematicians started to look at chaos and complexity.' He should know because he set up the Santa Fe Institute, which is the leading body in the world in the field of complexity.

Draw a dozen or so separated circles on a sheet of paper. Connect them up in any way you like. The only stipulation is that each circle has at least two lines coming from it. Now go around each circle and put a double slash on one of the merging lines and a single slash on another.

Start with any circle and exit by the line with the double slash. If you have entered by the double slash line you exit by the single slash line.

The circles represent 'neural states'. The line indicates that one state changes into the next state at the end of the connecting line. The double slash means that this is the preferred state of change. But if you enter from the preferred direction you need to exit along the second preference (because of the 'tiring' factor).

You will find that you always end up with a repeating cycle. This is what gives a thought or an idea a stable existence.

I once made a very simple computer model of the brain which had only five nerve cells. This brain was capable of fifty billion 'thoughts'. Any mathematician or electronic engineer would say this was nonsense. That is because they never consider the 'tiring factor'. This simply means that nerve cells, unlike transistors, get tired and their readiness to receive signals fluctuates. This process adds hugely increased complexity.

What it all amounts to is that the 'natural' behaviour of the brain is to set up stable patterns for dealing with a stable world. Only in this way is practical life possible.

• • •

Now the 'recognition thinking' of the Gang of Three emphasizes, enhances and builds upon this natural ability. The result is a very powerful method of thinking which has done very well for the human race in certain areas, such as science and technology, but rather poorly in other areas which require 'design' rather than judgement.

The Gang of Three built upon the natural behaviour of the brain.

While the brain is indeed excellent at pattern forming, recognition, judgement and discrimination, it is at the same time very poor at other activities, such as creativity.

If you have a racing car designed for speed on the circuit, then that car may not be good for shopping in a crowded town. The very excellence of a design in one direction may mean the inadequacy of the design in another direction.

I have preferred to focus upon those things which the brain is not set up to do. Rather than enhance what the brain does well I have set out to make it possible to think in ways the brain is not set up to think.

That is why I claim that the human race has never really learned to think. What we have is 'recognition', which is excellent and useful. But we have never developed the 'design' sort of thinking which we so badly need to design the future.

Once something is in a 'box' it is in the box – not half in and half out.

Once something is in a 'box' it is not easily free to be elsewhere.

Once something is in a 'box' it enjoys the full features of that 'box'.

When Lotfl Zadeh developed fuzzy logic in the USA in the 1970's, all the learned journals refused to publish anything to do with it.

They refused because fuzzy logic claims that something may be partly within a 'box' and partly outside the box. This claim directly contradicted Aristotle's second principle (in the box or out of the box) and so could not be accepted.

For fifteen hundred years people accepted that a heavy object would fall with a faster acceleration than a light object – because Aristotle had said so. Yet a simple twenty-second thought experiment would show that such behaviour is extremely unlikely.

The dominance of Aristotle's 'box thinking' is pervasive and powerful because it is so useful and so effective.

The result is that we tend to forget the dangers and limitations of the system.

Sit down and draw up a list of all the people you know quite well and with whom you have to interact. Write each name on a slip of paper.

Now take three waste paper baskets and label one of them 'friends'. Label the second one 'enemies'. Label the third one 'neutral'.

Take up the slips of paper one at a time and place each slip in one of the baskets. Would you find this easy to do? Would it require some thinking, and some compromises?

What about someone who was a sort of a friend but was capable of bad behaviour if the circumstances needed that?

What about someone who was a very weak 'friend'? Should that person be in the same box as a really good 'friend'?

Of course, it would be very much easier if we had multiple boxes. There would be a separate box for really good friends and another box for weak friends. There might even be a special box for 'half friend and half enemy'.

These multiple boxes would more closely reflect the reality of life. Usually, however, we do not do this; we stay with the basic boxes. This is largely because language only deals with basic boxes. Do we have a word for someone who is half friend and half enemy? This is not quite the same as a 'fair weather friend'.

In negotiations the basic boxes are very firmly set:

- Us vs them
- Friends vs enemies
- Our side vs the other side
- Good guys vs bad guys.

It is little wonder that we handle conflict so very badly. The emotions that are usually present in conflict situations – often for very good reasons – make the boxes even more basic and solid. Imagine that instead of boxes we had a spectrum. At one end of the spectrum there would be 'solid friend' and at the other end of the spectrum there would be 'solid enemy'. You could now place each person somewhere on that spectrum. If someone were near the middle, that person would relate both to the friend end and also the enemy end.

Unfortunately the human brain would find this 'spectrum system' impossible to work with.

Unfortunately language would not be able to cope with such a system.

Unfortunately the 'certainty' of logic could never operate in such a system.

So we are forced to perceive the world in a very inadequate way. We then act on those perceptions (perfectly logically) with very inadequate results. That is why the human race has never really learned to think.

Traditional, Aristotelian logic needs the certainty of boxes.

Boxes provide discrete entities to work with.

Boxes provide proven information linkages.

Two thousand years ago the Chinese were far ahead of the West in matters of science and technology. They had gunpowder, rockets, etc. Many basic inventions we take for granted originated in China.

So what happened? How did the West move ahead?

It seems that the Chinese never developed the key piece of mental software that is made up of the 'possibility system'.

It seems that they never developed the 'hypothesis' which is so essential in science.

The scholars wanted 'certainty' and they found certainty in descriptions: 'This is so.'

They got totally bogged down in the 'what is' system and never developed the 'what can be' system (creativity, design, hypothesis, etc.).

It is very much the same with our traditional logic system. In science the development of the hypothesis (a Greek invention) made a huge difference. In technology the development of 'possibilities' and 'vision' drives progress.

I do have to say, however, that in my experience of four of the major universities in the world (Oxford, Cambridge, London and Harvard), totally insufficient time is spent on the importance of hypotheses and the ability to generate these.

At one time a senior person in the French national research organization, CNRS, asked me whether I could help his scientists form hypotheses.

He told me: 'My scientists have been told that science is the analysis of data. That does not get you anywhere. They need to develop hypotheses to lead their thinking.'

Peptic ulcer is a rather important medical condition (stomach ulcers, duodenal ulcers, etc.). In the past, some people had to be on antacids for up to twenty years. There were rather fierce operations (Billroth 1, 2, 3, etc.) to remove part or all of the stomach. Many hospital beds were occupied by patients with such ulcers. The quality of life for these patients was not good.

Then a young doctor in Perth, Australia, had an idea that peptic ulcer was actually an 'infection'. Everyone laughed at him because the strong hydrochloric acid in the stomach would kill any bug. This young doctor was J.B. Marshall and he received the Nobel prize for Medicine in 2005 for his work.

Many years later, it turned out that he was right. Today the treatment is one week on antibiotics (possibly with bismuth) instead of twenty years on antacids or having your stomach removed.

We totally undervalue hypotheses and the whole 'possibility' system because logic has to work with certainty.

'Boxes' provide an apparent certainty of linkages. This can happen through general experience. All humans seem to die, so an apparent linkage in the 'human box' is mortality. If you judge that someone fits into the 'human box' then we can expect mortality of this person.

These certainties are based on packages of experience. No one has ever heard a snake singing so 'singing' is not part of the 'snake package' or box. But that is still a matter of experience.

A hundred years ago most people would have accepted that whales neither sing nor talk. Today, better instruments and research suggest that they both sing and talk. Certainty based on experience is only temporary – but usable none the less.

Then there is certainty based on 'definition'. If we define God as immortal, omnipotent and all-knowing, then that package is intact because only those beings that have all these characteristics could be called 'God'.

In a way, I am using that process myself in this book. If you defined thinking as any activity that takes place in the brain, then clearly the human race does think. If you define thinking as being good at recognizing 'what is' then the human race is rather good at thinking. But if you define thinking as including not only 'what is' but also 'what can be', then the human race has never really learned to think.

At its very best logic can never be better than its starting points. Godel set out to show that logic itself could never prove or justify these starting points. The starting points are provided by 'experience boxes' or 'definition boxes'.

The huge importance of perception will be discussed elsewhere in the book.

The immense practicality of the judgement/ recognition/ box system means that it will continue to be used – no matter how inadequate, and dangerous, it might be.

Imagine an early man walking through the jungle. He finds some red berries. He knows both from his own and from tribal experience that these berries are good to eat. He may even have a name for these good berries.

On another occasion he comes across some very similar red berries. But these new berries are very slightly different. He may recognize that these different berries actually fit in the 'poison' box. Even if he does not know this, he does know that they are not in the 'good berry box'. So he avoids them or is cautious, or even experiments with them.

For these very obvious 'survival' reasons, the brain has a powerful natural 'mis-match' mechanism. If something is experienced which is different from what is known and expected, the brain is very good at picking out the difference.

So with the 'box-labelling' system and the mis-match mechanism, the brain is equipped to cope with a stable world.

In most courts of law the verdict at the end is 'innocent' or 'guilty'. There are obvious practical reasons for this. What are you going to do with the accused?

The simple two-box system is very practical. Either there is enough evidence, 'beyond a reasonable doubt' in criminal cases, to secure a guilty verdict or there is not. In civil cases it is the 'balance' of evidence that secures a conviction.

Scottish courts have long had a third 'box'. This third box is labelled 'not proven'. This means that the accused has not been proved to be guilty but this does not mean that the accused is thereby innocent. The case can be re-opened at any time, whereas in other countries the 'double jeopardy' law prevents re-trial for the same offence.

Interestingly, the British courts are now adopting the Scottish principle. The reason is that future technology may make it possible to re-examine the evidence and secure a conviction. For example, refined DNA technology might show that someone acquitted of a murder twenty years ago was actually guilty.

In this example, advancing technology has shown the limitations of the traditional boxes.

In the USA as much as ninety-five per cent of criminal cases are settled by 'plea-bargaining'. Such cases are never tried in court. It saves a lot of time and expense. In the end, the guilty party knows that he or she is guilty. So a person accused of murder might be persuaded to accept a verdict of 'manslaughter'. It is just possible that innocent people might be pressured to accept lesser charges rather than face the court on the full initial charge. At the same time such people are no worse off than if plea-bargaining were not a possibility – they would be facing the court anyway.

I mention plea-bargaining here because it is a very different approach from the 'innocent' or 'guilty' boxes determined by the judgment of the court.

For this and many other reasons, there are six times as many people in prison in the USA (per 1000 of the population) than in Europe.

A teacher in school marks a pupil's work as 'right' or 'wrong'. If the pupil provides the expected answer then this is marked 'right'. Anything else is 'wrong'. This means that pupils spend their time trying to guess what answer the teacher wants. This completely kills creativity and originality. At the same time we need to acknowledge the practicality of the system.

If there were no standard 'right' or 'wrong' answers, then it would all depend on the personal judgement of the teacher. This might work very well with gifted teachers. But it would be a disaster with other teachers where personal whim or idiosyncrasy would totally confuse the pupils. We might, however, plead for a box called 'interesting'. An answer which was different from the standard expected answer could still be judged 'interesting'.

In the CoRT Thinking Programme designed for schools there is a very simple 'attention-directing' tool called the PMI. This asks the students to look first at the Plus points in the situation and then at the Minus points. The 'I' stands for Interesting. This is because there are many points which are neither good nor bad but worthy of being noticed.

So the design of 'new boxes' can help to overcome the limitations of the usual recognition system.

'Truth' would be a silly joke if it were not such a dangerous one.

Yet 'truth' is the basis of our beliefs, our thinking, our actions and our philosophy.

To challenge our traditional concept of 'truth' does not mean that one is therefore in favour of 'untruth'. Such a simple assumption illustrates the limitations of our 'box' system. If you are not in the 'truth' box then you must be in the 'untruth' box.

If you are against 'dirty water', does that mean that you are in favour of 'pure water'? Not at all.

You might be very much against dirty water but very much in favour of Coca-Cola, tea, lemonade, etc., none of which are 'pure water'.

If you ask someone the way to the river and that person tells you the wrong way (intentionally), that is not a good thing.

If someone asks you if there is any beer in the refrigerator and you say there is not, when a six-pack of Fosters is staring at you, that is not a good thing.

If a smitten young lady asks the fellow if he is married and he says he is not, then that is not a good thing if he is indeed married.

If you calculate the weight a bridge can carry and get it wrong, then that is not a good thing because the bridge will collapse.

It is not hard to see how 'truth' is so essential to human affairs and therefore so very highly valued.

At the same time this powerful concept can be dangerous and misleading.

The newspaper billboard announced in large type: 'Teacher stabbed'. Being aware of the increasing violence in schools, I bought the paper to find out what had happened, and also for an update on violence in schools.

It turned out that a man walking along the road had been stabbed by a mugger. It was nothing whatever to do with classrooms, school or education. The man might have been a plumber, a lawyer, a pizza delivery man or anyone else.

Yet the statement 'Teacher stabbed' was absolutely true − and totally misleading at the same time. Was this misleading intentional? It is difficult to be sure but I doubt if the composer of that billboard would have been content with: 'Man stabbed'. The use of the word 'teacher' was surely deliberate. If it sells papers, who cares?

● ● ●

There are many different sorts of truth which are bundled together under the heading 'truth', all of which claim that absolute rightness.

There is 'tested truth'. If I weigh this bar of gold it weighs one kilogram. The measuring scales indicate that. Any properly functioning scales would also show one kilogram. This actually means that the bar weighs as much as the standard one kilogram weight kept in Paris. All properly functioning scales would need to show one kilogram when tested against this standard bar − or substitutes.

It follows that I need to have complete faith in the testing apparatus.

In medicine there are some tests which, in a small minority of cases, might show a false positive or a false negative. So a person with cancer might be told she does not have cancer. And a person with no cancer might be told that she does have cancer. This only happens in a tiny number of cases.

If you look at a plate and see two apples on it then the testing apparatus is your eye. Anyone else with properly functioning eyes would see the same two apples.

When people tell you about their experience you are not using their testing apparatus (like the eye) directly. The person might have experienced an illusion. The person's memory might be faulty. When children were asked about their childhood, several falsely accused a parent of abuse. This was not deliberate but memory had constructed a scenario which never existed. The person might also be deliberately deceitful.

The whole purpose of 'scientific truth' is to get rid of most of these difficulties and to show that the same tests applied by many different people will produce the same results. What scientists do not always understand is that this validity of testing does not equally apply to the interpretation of the results. The interpretation of results is more individual and relies on individual hypotheses and frameworks which have not themselves been tested.

In science, proof is often no more than lack of imagination. We are sure that B must have been caused by A simply because we cannot imagine any other cause. So many errors in science have arisen just from this obvious limitation.

With 'general experience' truth we accept as true what most people claim to have experienced. This gets rid of the problem of personal deceit, personal faulty memory and personal illusion. What it does not get rid of is 'selective perception'.

The patterns formed in the brain ensure that the brain perceives what it is most ready to perceive. This gives rise to prejudice, stereotypes, discrimination, etc. If there is an existing prejudice that people from the land of Palia tend to be thieves, then you will particularly notice any thieving behaviour by Palians. You will not notice that ninety-eight per cent of Palians are not thieves. You will not notice that thieving among Palians is not higher than among any other ethnic group. It is for these reasons that newspapers in many countries are forbidden to give the ethnic origin of arrested criminals unless this is directly relevant.

Truth based on selective perception is one of the most dangerous forms of truth because it is genuinely experienced and genuinely believed to be true.

Truth based on selective perception is a particular form of 'belief truth'. Here we set up a framework of beliefs and values. Looking at the world through that framework reinforces the 'truth' of that framework. Religious beliefs are of this type.

Unfortunately, in order to confirm the 'truth' of your beliefs you may need to show that other belief systems are 'not true'. Historically, this has meant war, persecutions, pog-roms, etc.

The Moslems accept Christians and Jews as 'people of the book'. They consider that Islam is the latest edition of the same 'book' or religion. This may explain why, historically, Moslems were much less inclined to persecute Christians or Jews in Moslem cities than the other way around. If you are confident you have less need to prove yourself right.

Then there is 'game truth'. Because this is totally artificial it is, in a sense, the truest form of truth. In chess, because you have agreed to 'play the game' the queen piece cannot jump over other pieces.

This is a false, disallowed or 'untrue' move. In the game of soccer a player is not allowed to pick up the ball, run with it and place it in the opponent's goal. This is a false or 'untrue' move. In the game of rugby, however, the rules are different and you are permitted to pick up the ball and run with it. Once you accept the game then you 'play the rules'.

Mathematics is a classic example of 'game truth'. You set up the game or universe and then see where the rules get you. The rules vary with the universe. Euclidean geometry is a different game from spherical geometry and the rules are different in a spherical universe. The immense usefulness of mathematics is that we can apply these game rules to the world around with the same certainty of truth – that is why bridges do not often fall down.

Logic as such is a classic example of 'game truth'. You need to follow the rules of logic which are said to apply to all human thinking. There is, however, one very important distinction that is almost always overlooked.

If you have four square tiles how do you arrange them to give a bigger square? If you have four triangular pieces, how do you arrange them to give a square? Logic works very well with the starting concepts. But where do these come from? Not from logic itself, nor can they be tested with logic (Godel). The starting pieces come from 'perceptual choice'. The logic may be perfect but if the starting perceptions are faulty the result will be rubbish.

Most often the starting pieces are 'words' in a language. Those words package general experience or perception and have no validity beyond this. Perception is quite likely to be selective or faulty.

David Perkins in the education department at Harvard showed

that ninety per cent of the errors in non-technical thinking were errors of perception and not of logic at all. Perception might be egocentric, narrow, limited in time, poor in options, etc.

It is one of the great tragedies and mistakes of history to assume that excellent logic will justify poor starting perceptions. Yet it is easy to see how this came about.

At the Renaissance most thinkers were theologians. There was no such thing as 'personal perception'. There were given concepts, such as God is all knowing, God is omnipotent, etc. You worked with these 'given pieces' with excellent logic and so set out to prove heretics wrong. The assumption was that this was 'game truth'. It was indeed game truth but only if you believed in that game and accepted all the starting pieces.

There is a little problem that upsets quite a lot of people. In a television show the guest answers the questions correctly and so the host asks the guest to choose between three doors. Behind one door is a Porsche car which goes to the guest if the guest chooses that door. Behind the other doors are goats. We can call them doors A, B and C. The host asks the guest to make a provisional choice. The guest chooses door A.

The host now routinely opens another door, door C, to reveal a goat. The host then asks the guest if he or she is happy with door A or would like to shift to door B.

The correct answer is that the guest doubles his or her chance of getting the car if he or she does shift to door B.

This answer upsets many people – even top mathematicians. Yet a slight change in 'perception' shows why the answer is obvious.

Perception is undoubtedly the biggest source of false truth. The trouble is that many different perceptions may all be equally right, valid or true. The danger is that those who hold one perception as true are reluctant to accept the possible truth of other perceptions.

In mathematics adding four to four gives the figure eight. There is no doubt about such 'game truth'. But if you then claim that eight is made up of four added to four then that is not a unique truth. There is seven added to one, six added to two and five added to three. All of these are equally valid perceptions.

'Description truth' has always been extremely dangerous as a form of perceptual truth. You could describe a walking stick as made up of a shaft and a handle. Someone else wants a more 'complete' description and talks about the handle, the middle piece and the end piece. Then the next person introduces 'linking pieces' between the handle and the middle piece, and between the middle piece and the end piece.

There is no limit to the variety of descriptions and all of them are 'true' in the sense that they are valid. The trouble arises when you start believing that if your description is true then other descriptions must be false.

● ● ●

We could introduce the concept of 'pragmatism' at this point. Which of the many descriptions is the most 'useful' (as suggested by William James)? At this point we are moving away from the concept of 'truth'.

How many people travelling 'North' actually want to reach the North Pole? 'North' is a useful direction in which to be travelling. In a very similar way, 'truth' is excellent as a direction in which to be thinking. The danger arises when we claim truth as a destination.

'We have the truth and therefore anything different is not the truth.'

Truth is a very useful and usable notion provided it is a direction. Truth becomes both silly and dangerous when we claim its absolute nature.
We could introduce a concept of a 'proto-truth'. A proto-truth is a truth we hold to be true provided we are trying to change it.

When a kitchen appliance is labelled as 'complying with safety standards' then we feel safe in using that appliance. In the same way the label of 'truth' is applied to so many things with the intention of saying: 'Trust us. This is what you should believe.'

In traditional logic you move from one certainty to another. A string of 'maybe' links would never have the same force.

Perception is by far the most important part of thinking. It has also always been the most neglected.

We have believed and taught that logic is enough.

At best, logic can only service our perceptions.

Imagine that you had never seen a motor car before. Suddenly, before your eyes there is this stationary motor car.

There is this strange shiny object with round things at each end. You know very little about it, what it does, why it may be useful.

For most people it is impossible to get back to that 'innocent' position.

We know that motor cars move and carry people. We know that they work on petrol (or diesel) and that they travel along roads. We may even know the make of this particular car. We may know someone who has a similar car. All these are matters that the brain brings to our physical experience of the car.

In some cases it is possible to restore the sight of people who have been born blind. Apparently it takes such people quite a long time to 'learn' to see.

Perception is the interaction of the brain with the environment. There may be the perception of the moment as we see or hear something. There may also be the 'perception' of an internal thought: a problem, a project or a situation.

There is a lone antique shop on the road. Then another antique shop opens across the street. One of the two partners who own the first shop complains that this is going to provide competition and will hurt the business. The other partner perceives it differently. The other partner welcomes the new shop and even hopes that more antique shops will open in the same street. In this way it will become an 'antiques district' and people will come to the street to look for antiques.

As a result of the different perceptions the behaviour of the two partners will be quite different. The first partner may look to sell out his share in the shop. The second partner might be motivated to buy this share.

The actual situation is exactly the same for both partners. It is what the brain brings to the actual situation that creates the different perceptions.

The very word 'perception' is not very satisfactory. It can be used to refer to what we actually see (or hear or feel) at the moment. It can also be used to include all the brain activity that brings understanding, experience and motivation to connect with what we actually see at the moment.

Although we do accept the importance of perception we have never done anything about it. The reasons are fairly obvious.

● ● ●

The power of mathematics fascinated thinkers who loved its certainty. Logic was an attempt to apply the same formality and certainty to ordinary thinking.

At the Renaissance there was the re-introduction of Greek and Roman thinking into Europe. The people who were most interested in this wonderful 'new thinking' were theologians, humanists and lawyers. All of these groups were interested in 'argument' and seeking to prove a point. So the processing aspect of logic got emphasized and developed.

Very little attention was paid to perception because it was so variable and so intangible. People saw things as they were told to see them – not as a matter of individual idiosyncrasy. In any case, in theology, the starting concepts were already fixed and it was a matter of arguing around these.

If you are playing around with words then it is difficult to get an understanding of perception.

Today, however, we can begin to understand the nature of the brain as a self-organizing information system, as described in an earlier part of this book. We can see how the brain forms patterns. We can see how perception works. From this basis we can begin to design 'thinking tools' that help improve perception.

● ● ●

For some years now, there has been a 'one child' policy in China. This means that families are only permitted to have one child. Families want to have a son to look after them in their old age, since a daughter goes to the husband's family. As a result girl children are aborted, abandoned or given up for adoption. As a result of all this there is now a shortage of one hundred million women in China.

Suppose there was a different approach. Every family would be allowed to have as many children as they liked – until they had a boy and then they would stop having children. What would happen?

There would be many families with more than one girl – even some with as many as six girls. But no family could have more than one boy.

At first sight it seems obvious that there would be many more girls in the population than boys.

Then we shift 'attention' and change our perception. At the moment of conception there is an equal chance of their being a boy or a girl. This cannot be altered. So equal numbers of boys and girls are conceived and born. No baby is being killed. The end result is a balanced boy/girl population and somewhat less than replacement in numbers (giving a diminishing population).

If you are not looking in a certain direction you will not see what lies in that direction no matter how excellent your vision might be.

Attention flows of its own accord.

Attention may also be directed deliberately.

There is a type of thinking called 'point-to-point' thinking. This means that at any point you take the easiest connection to the next point.

Twenty-four groups of youngsters in schools ranging from the elite to the disadvantaged were given the same question: 'Would it be a good idea if bread, fish and meat were to be free?'

Twenty-three of the groups decided it would not be a good idea. The thinking went as follows.

…If these things were free everyone would want them.

…The shops would be crowded.
…The buses going to the shops would be crowded.

…The drivers on the buses would ask for higher wages.

…The drivers would not get the higher wages so they would go on strike.

…This strike would hurt everyone.

…So it would not be a good idea.

This is typical point-to-point thinking. It is possible that at the time there was also some strike that introduced this element into the thinking.

Attention flows in the same way. We move from one point to the next most obvious point. Attention flows naturally unless there is some particular matter which catches our attention.

But attention can also be directed in a deliberate and formal way.

An expert is someone who has learned to direct his or her attention to the really important aspects of the situation in which the expertise occurs.

A good physician knows exactly what to pay attention to when examining a patient. A good medical professor on his or her ward rounds carefully directs the attention of the students.

'Notice how that patient is breathing.'

'Notice the raised pressure in the jugular vein.'

'Observe the fingers on that patient.'

Teaching art appreciation is also a matter of directing attention.

'Notice the composition.'

'Look at the choice of colours.'

'Observe the brushwork.'

'See the careful use of light and shade.'

Many people have seen El Greco paintings but have not noticed something peculiar about the fingers on the figure of Christ. Typically, the third and fourth fingers are widely separated. This was considered a mark of holiness.

We cannot notice, observe or pay attention to everything around us. So what we choose to pay attention to is very important since that will determine our perception and in turn our behaviour.

The CoRT Thinking Programme, which is now widely used in thousands of schools world wide, offers a series of very simple 'attention-directing' tools. The student practices the tools and learns to use them deliberately in a variety of different thinking situations.

The PMI tool has already been mentioned. Another simple tool is the OPV. Here the thinker formally directs attention to the thinking of the other people involved in the situation (Other People's Views). It is that simple.

In the South African mine a fight started between two underground locomotive drivers. Both of them had taken the 'thinking course'. So one of them suggested they 'do an OPV'. They did and the dispute simply dissolved. There are many other examples of this.

In a prominent British Sunday paper one very well-known critic observed that simply putting the term 'OPV' on the operation of looking at other people's views did nothing. This is a wonderful example of the arrogant stupidity of some people and of newspapers. Writers pontificate with great assurance on matters about which they know virtually nothing. This is from the absurd notion that a well-educated mind can think about anything. Writers certainly cannot be expert in all matters but they can ask questions instead of pontificating in so ridiculous a manner.

The actual difference between 'doing an OPV' and having the attitude of looking at other people's views is huge. This can be seen over and again in real classrooms with real students – not sitting back and pontificating with total absurdity.

The difference is that attitudes are very difficult to build up, to transfer and to use. Capturing the attitude with a formal and deliberate tool makes all the difference. The tool now has an entity. The tool exists and has a location in the brain just as the concept of 'ice-cream' or 'motor car' has a location. The tool is now usable in any situation.

The story also illustrates how the infantile arrogance and presumptions of the press have a seriously negative effect on the thinking of society.

Another simple tool is the C&S, which encourages the thinker to look at the Consequences and Sequels.

I was once addressing a meeting of two hundred and fifty top women executives. I suggested that women should be paid fifteen per cent more than men for doing the same job.

Eighty-five per cent of those present liked the idea and even said that it 'was about time too'.

I then explained the C&S in about three minutes and asked them to apply this attention-directing tool to the suggestion.

When they had done this, the percentage in favour dropped from eighty-five to just fifteen.

Now every one of those senior executives was used to looking at consequences in her usual work. That is what executives do all the time. Every person would have been insulted had I suggested that they did not consider the consequences of actions or decisions.

But introducing the c&s tool in a very deliberate and formal manner made a huge difference, even to those intelligent and highly educated people.

None of this is at all surprising. If you say to someone: 'Look around you', then that person notices the more prominent things. If you say to the same person: 'Look West and tell me what you see', then you get much more detail.

North, South, East and West are useful spatial directions in which to look or to move. The attention-directing tools provide convenient ways to direct our attentions.

Regrettably, some academics hate simplicity because it deprives them of the special importance of complexity. One Canadian academic sat in his office and gave the opinion that these 'simple tools' could not work. But they do work – with thousands of teachers world wide. You can sit in an office and say that cheese cannot exist. But cheese does exist.

There is a very big difference between description and action.

Unfortunately, most of our attention to thinking has been in the form of description, analysis, reflection and philosophical examination.

None of these approaches provide simple, practical and effective operational tools for thinking.

For more than two thousand years we have been content with argument as a way of examining a subject.
This is a crude and primitive method of thinking that emphasizes 'case making' rather than exploration.

We have been content to use such an inefficient method in politics, in law, in business and even in domestic affairs. Why?

Consider a court of law in the USA or in the UK. If the prosecuting lawyer thinks of a point which would help the defence case is he or she going to bring up that point? If the defence lawyer thinks of a point which would help the prosecution case, would he or she bring up that point? In both cases the answer is a definite 'No'.

The purpose of such a court of law is not 'exploration' of the subject but 'case making'.

Argument is part of the thinking idiom of 'what is'. One side of the argument claims that it 'is' something; the other side claims that it 'is' something else. The argument then takes place to see who is right.

Occasionally, there is a synthesis of both points of view. More often, one party or other believes that it has won the argument.

One day a man painted the left hand side of his car white and the right hand side black. His friends asked him why he did this strange thing. He replied: 'Whenever I have an accident, it is such fun to hear the witnesses in court contradict each other.'

This is typical of argument. Each side believes it is absolutely right but is actually only looking at one part of the situation.

● ● ●

If argument is so primitive why do we still use it?
The first answer is that for over two thousand years we have not designed something better than argument.

The second answer is historical. Socrates developed argument as a way of thinking about a subject. Aristotle with his judgement and 'box certainties' provided a powerful methodology.

The Renaissance brought this thinking back into Europe. The thinkers and educators of the time were mainly church people. What did these people need from thinking?

They needed ways of proving heretics to be 'wrong' and they needed ways of reassuring themselves of their own beliefs. Argument fitted this need perfectly.

There was no room for synthesis, design or compromise. The Church had to be right and the heretics had to be wrong – so they could be burned at the stake.

The Church needed the absolutism of Plato and the argument of Aristotle – perhaps rather more than the questioning of Socrates. Other Greek thinkers, including the Sophists, were ignored.

Argument is intended to give a defined end point: one party has won and the other has lost. This defined end-point was attractive in law.

Argument replaced 'trial by combat' in which the 'champion' of the state would fight the alleged criminal. There would be but one winner. Argument was a combat with words rather than swords.

• • •

Four people are standing around a chateau. Each one insists that the side he or she faces is the best side. They argue (by mobile phone). In the end they all join up and walk around the building so each person is now seeing all the sides. Such behaviour leads directly to the concept of 'parallel thinking'.

The big difference between parallel thinking and adversarial thinking (argument) is that at any moment everyone is thinking in parallel. Everyone is thinking and looking in the same direction. The directions then change so all aspects of the matter are eventually covered.

The whole point of parallel thinking is that everyone is thinking about the subject matter not about what the other person has said. For this reason there is a thorough exploration of the subject and, usually, some agreed way forward at the end.

If everyone were to think and to look in the same direction there would need to be some clearly indicated direction. This direction is provided by the symbolic 'Six Hats'. At any one moment everyone is wearing, metaphorically, one of the six hats. So everyone ends up thinking in the same direction.

The White Hat symbolizes 'information'. Think of white and paper. Under the White Hat everyone is focusing on information.

- What information do we have?
- What information do we need?
- Questions we want to ask...
- How do we get the information we want?

If there is disagreement, there is no argument. Both differing versions are recorded.

The Red Hat is for emotions, feelings and intuition. Think red and fire and warmth. Under the Red Hat everyone has permission to put forward his or her emotions, feelings and intuition without having to explain or justify these. They exist in a person and so can be put forward. Before the first election in South Africa they asked me to teach the method to the heads of the Peace Accord Committees. They then chose to use the Red Hat as the first hat in a meeting: to allow everyone to express his or her feelings right at the beginning.

- What do I feel about this?
- My intuition is as follows...
- I have this feeling...
- I am very angry about this...
- There are many doubts...

The Black Hat is for thinking that is cautious, careful and critical. Think of black and a judge's robes. Under the Black Hat we think of the 'downside'; why something may not work; what the potential problems might be. This is the 'critical' hat.

- Does this fit our budget?
- Is this ethical?
- Will this work?
- What can go wrong?
- What are the risks?

Under the Black Hat, thinkers are encouraged to be as cautious and negative as possible. This fits both the natural behaviour of the brain and also a critical thinking culture. The Black Hat is an excellent hat and probably the most important of the hats. It is also the basis of Western thinking culture. But it can be over-used by those who believe it is enough to be critical.

The Yellow Hat is for the 'logical positive'. Under the Yellow Hat we look for the values and benefits. We look to see how something can be done. All this does have to be reasonable – it is not the speculation of creativity. In all constructive thinking it is important to develop 'value sensitivity'. We have a natural 'danger sensitivity' but we have to develop 'value sensitivity'.

- What are the values here?
- What are the benefits?
- How can this be done?
- What are the positive aspects?

The Yellow Hat is much harder and much less 'natural' than the Black Hat.

The Green Hat is the hat of creativity and energy. Think 'green' and vegetation and growth. Under the Green Hat everyone present at the meeting makes a creative effort. This is the time and place for creativity. Under the Green Hat we look for fresh ideas, alternative, modifications of an idea, possibilities, etc.

- Here is another alternative...
- We could change the idea...
- We could also do this...
- There are these possibilities...
- What new approach might there be?

In ordinary thinking the critical mode is available at every moment. Under the Green Hat it is formally excluded.

The last hat is the Blue Hat. Think blue and sky and overview. The Blue Hat organizes the thinking. The Blue Hat decides on the focus. The Blue Hat decides the sequence of hats to be used. The Blue Hat enforces the discipline of the hats. The Blue Hat puts together outcomes, solutions, designs, next steps, etc.

- What are we thinking about?
- What do we want to achieve?
- What is the outcome here?
- Can we suggest a solution?
- What is the next step?

This surprisingly simple framework can be very powerful. Meeting times can be reduced to one quarter or even one tenth of their usual time.

What is most important is that each thinker is challenged to use all his or her experience, information and 'brain power'. It is totally different from 'clever case making'.

A major oil company had a problem with a drilling rig that was costing them one hundred thousand dollars a day. They had been thinking about it for some time. Then Jens Arup, a certified trainer in the method, introduced the Six Hats. In twelve minutes they had reached a solution which saved them ten million dollars.

In Thailand Rasmee Tanyatorn introduced the Six Hats to a meeting of a construction firm that was facing severe performance penalties. In a few hours they had designed a way forward which saved them twenty million baht.

The hats may be used individually to request a type of thinking.

When Ron Barbaro was president of Prudential Insurance he might suggest an idea. Those around would point out the dangers and why the idea might not work. He would listen and then say: 'That is great Black Hat thinking, now I would like the Yellow Hat.'

Normally, if someone is against an idea that person is not going to put forward the virtues of the idea. But with Six Hats thinking, the person is challenged to do exactly this.

Suppose you are against an idea. Under the Black Hat you are invited to put forward all the concern and caution points. Then it is the turn of the Yellow Hat. You are now invited to focus on the value of the idea. If you declare that you cannot see any value while everyone around is spelling out the values – then you appear to be stupid. If the values are there, why can you not see them? So you look for value and sometimes surprise yourself in the process.

The parallel thinking of the Six Hats is a very powerful process. It does, however, need to be used properly otherwise the power of the process is wasted. Formal training and the certification of instructors can be arranged through APTT in Iowa.

The hats may be used singly in order to request a specific type of thinking:

'Give me your Red Hat on this.'

The hats may also be used in a formal sequence. There are guidelines to the setting up of a sequence and these guidelines are part of the training.

In practice, people find the process to be very liberating. A thinker is no longer trapped in one mode (for or against the idea). In Japan the hats give thinkers permission to be creative, or critical or to express their feelings.

The method is used equally by four year olds in school and by top executives at some of the world's largest corporations.

• • •

Experience over many years has shown that the process is easy to learn and to use (if done properly). It is powerful in its effects and obtains the full power of the minds of those at the meeting.

We then need to ask why it has taken two thousand four hundred years to come up with such a simple framework.

The answer is that ever since the Gang of Three we have believed that argument was the ideal form of discussion. There is also the point, mentioned earlier, that Church thinkers at the Renaissance were not interested in exploring a subject but only in proving heretics to be wrong. Imagine a parliament which used the Six Hats instead of the usual bickering and point scoring!

What is particularly interesting about the Six Hats method is that once the subject has been thoroughly explored the 'way forward' often becomes obvious to everyone at the meeting. It is no longer a matter of arguing one proposal against another, or of voting. When the 'road map' has been laid out clearly, it is easy to pick the right road.

There is another, physiological, reason why the Six Hats may be necessary.

A zebra in Africa hears a rustle in the grass nearby. Immediately all the nerve cell clusters in the zebra's brain that are concerned with danger are alerted (stimulated), so when the lion appears the zebra can react immediately.

Research is beginning to show that brain chemicals sensitize certain areas according to the overall emotional need. So when we are frightened we do see more danger; when we are positive we do see more value, etc. Since we cannot be 'sensitized' in all directions at the same time, we need to separate out our thinking modes – as is done with the Six Hats, where each type of thinking is separated out and given full attention.

Consider the messiness of normal thinking or argument. At one moment we are being critical. At another moment we are searching for information. At another moment we are trying to be creative. All this is mixed in together. It is like trying to juggle with six balls at a time instead of just tossing one ball at a time.

Why is there this obsession with history?

Universities and Western intellectual culture are obsessed with history.

This obsession with history means that far too little effort is put into designing the way forward.

'If you do not learn the mistakes of history you are doomed to repeat them.'

SANTAYANA

'If you learn the successes of history you are doomed to be trapped by them.'

DE BONO

At the Renaissance scholars, academics and intellectuals, in general, realized that there was a great deal to be learned by looking backwards at Greek and Roman thinking, civilization and culture.

In fact there was far more to be learned by looking backwards than by looking around or looking forward.

This was a very reasonable attitude at the time. Unfortunately universities have never recovered from this attitude. Far too much time is spent studying history in almost any subject area.

There is another, even more basic, reason why we are obsessed with history.

Scholars are people who know and people who study. What is there to know? What is there to study?

In science you can seek to study how things work and why things happen. In mathematics you can explore further the game of mathematics. But in almost every other subject area the only thing to study and the only thing about which you can have superior knowledge is history.

History is there. History is available to be studied. History is waiting to be studied. You can study history in great detail. Students can be set to study history.

It is fair to pay homage to the great minds of the past in any area

– but the practical relevance of these minds to today's needs may be tiny. In psychology do you really need to know the thinking of all the great psychologists of the past?

If you are not particularly creative you can get far through hard work and application in the field of history. You can research and collate better than anyone else. This is admirable.

It would be unfair to claim that historians are not creative because many are creative. At the same time you can get very far in history without any need to be creative.

Is there anything wrong with this obsession with history? There is one main problem. This obsession takes up time, money, resources, space, etc. and crowds out other subjects which are as important – and even more important – than history. How many universities give as much time, space, money and resources to 'design' as to history?

With history you know what will be done. With history you know the 'scholarly' outcome that will result. This is not at all so with 'design'. There may be no outcome at all. The outcome may be trite or ridiculous. It is not difficult to see why history is a preferred academic choice.

There is also the matter of 'apostolic succession'. Existing history departments produce excellent historians who can carry on working with history. There are very few 'design' departments to produce those who can run design departments. So we are locked into a continuity that can diverge further and further from the real needs of society.

How many universities have chairs, faculties or departments of 'thinking'? Yet 'thinking' is every bit as important to society as is history.

Most academics would not even consider 'thinking' as a subject in its own right. Now the history of thinking would be a different matter. Unfortunately, learning the history of thinking is of no practical help whatsoever if you have to do some real thinking in the real world.

By definition all knowledge comes from the past. It may be the past of five minutes ago or five centuries ago.

Surely this is enough justification for history?

There is knowledge and there is what we do with knowledge. In its origin a motor car was put together from existing knowledge. To that knowledge had to be added engineering skill and design.

There are very few situations where pure knowledge as such is sufficient. So if we spend so much time on history for the sake of the knowledge it may deliver, surely we should spend an almost equal amount of time on the 'use' of knowledge in designing ways forward.

We come back to the front left wheel analogy. I have nothing against the front left wheel of a motor car but I would have a problem with anyone who believed that a front left wheel was enough. In the same way I believe history to be very useful. It is the obsession with history – at the expense of other areas – that I believe to be a danger.

DE BONO'S LAW

'Any system with an input of information spaced out over time, and the periodic need to make the best use of available information, will always be sub-optimal.'

(Because the sequence of arrival of the information plays too large a part in its disposition.)

You are given two cardboard pieces as shown in the diagram (on page 57). The task is to put them together to give a simple coherent shape that could easily be described over the telephone in such a way that the person at the other end of the telephone could reproduce your shape.

You think for a bit and then you put the pieces together to give a rectangle, as shown. You might go further and describe the rectangle as being three times as long as it is wide.

You are now given another piece. This is the small square as shown. It is obvious, easy and logical to add the square to the end of the rectangle to give a longer rectangle (now four times as long as it is wide).

Finally, you are given two longer pieces as shown. You might try to arrange them alongside the existing rectangle. Unfortunately they do not fit.

In order to go forward, you now have to go back to change an arrangement which seemed the best at the time. You alter the second arrangement to give a square. The new pieces can now be added to give a bigger square, as shown below.

FIGURE I

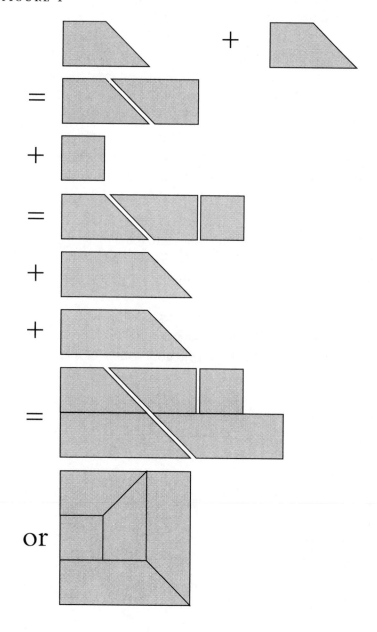

This simple demonstration shows a very important principle. This is the principle defined in 'de Bono's law'.

Because you were given the first two pieces the best arrangement was indeed the rectangle.

Had you been given the small square first you might well have arranged the pieces as a square – and the next step would have been easy. The sequence of arrival of the pieces (of information) determines the way the information is put together.

On the arrival of the small square if you had arranged the pieces as a square then the future might have given you a smaller rectangle and you would have been better off with the rectangle.

In other words, it does not matter how smart you are, there will always be a need to go back and change a concept, an idea, an arrangement which in its day was the best possible one.

The implications of this simple understanding are huge. It means that the best progress is not in a linear evolutionary line. We may need to go back and change concepts which in their day were very good – but now block the way to better concepts.

This 'sequence effect' is also the logical basis for creativity and shows why creativity is not a luxury but essential.

The simple demonstration illustrated above is not strictly a 'self-organizing' system because the person arranging the pieces is doing the organizing. But exactly the same principle applies to self-organizing systems where the pieces arrange themselves to give the best arrangement 'at the moment'.

Self-organizing systems reach stable local arrangements. In order to go further, and to make use of the knowledge available, it may be necessary to disturb this 'local equilibrium' in order to reach a more 'global equilibrium'. There are now mathematical papers showing the necessity for this.

The process is sometimes called 'annealing'. When you make steel, the crystals lock into a stable position when the steel cools down. This position is stable but not very strong. You may have to heat the steel again (a form of provocation) so that the crystals can lock more tightly to give a stronger steel. You may do this again and again.

What it means is that 'stable positions' (local equilibriums) are not necessarily the best positions.

Unfortunately, moving out of the stable position to start to move to a better position is extremely difficult. This is because any first steps are seen to be negative when compared to the existing stability which creates its own framework of judgement (and guardians to enforce that judgement).

That is why Einstein said that any new idea would be greeted with violent opposition. This has certainly been my own experience. The guardians of the status quo resent any change. This is especially so if they do not even understand the suggested change.

In the world of art, the painter Turner was initially treated with derision but is today amongst the most revered English artists. In France, the first impressionists, and cubists in their turn, were also met by fierce opposition.

This difficulty of moving away from a stable local equilibrium does lead to greater stability in society. It also means that progress is much slower than it needs to be.

We always hope that change will be by small, slow steps that do not upset anyone. Sometimes this is indeed possible. Usually it is not.

Understanding of the behaviour of self-organizing systems and of 'de Bono's law' might help in encouraging change.

Of course, there are times when a new idea has been created but the perceived cost of change is too high and so we continue with the old idea even though it is far from the best.

You are climbing a mountain and it is very foggy. You reach the top of the mountain but your altimeter shows the wrong height. You realize that you have climbed to the top of a subsidiary peak. To reach the real peak you have to go back and start again. It is often the same with ideas.

But we cannot allow ourselves to accept the implications of this. We fool ourselves that progress happens in a linear fashion.

Our thinking about creativity has always been muddled, feeble and stupid.

This is not surprising.

I once found it necessary to invent the new word 'crazytivity'.

There are people who believe that 'being different for the sake of being different is creativity'. It is not. At the end of the creative process there has to be a value.

If someone suggests making triangular, rather than the usual rectangular doors, then unless some value can be shown for the triangular doors, that is 'crazytivity'.

Normally we would set out to reach some 'end value' through a step-by-step, logical process. We acknowledge, however, that sometimes an end value is produced by a process other than the step-by-step logical one. We therefore give this 'mysterious' process the name of creativity.

A simple definition of creativity is 'unexpected effectiveness'. There is the value of effectiveness. At the same time the idea was not expected.

A big problem arises with the word 'creative' – at least in the English language.

'To create means to bring something into being' – so would creating a mess be regarded as creative?

An artist brings into being a painting which is seen to have value. So we call the artist creative. Something has been 'created' so the person responsible is creative.

With 'found art' the artist may not have made anything but may have applied his or her aesthetic sense to found objects such as driftwood, rocks, etc.

Failure to distinguish between artistic creativity and idea creativity has caused huge problems.

We come to believe that since artistic genius cannot be taught then creativity is an in-born talent and cannot be developed as a skill. This is rubbish.

We come to believe that teaching youngsters in school to dance or play music is teaching them creativity. This is also rubbish.

We come to believe that creativity is a mystery that can never be understood. This is major rubbish.

So we do nothing.

There are many artists, especially musicians, who use my work. Nevertheless, I have been interested in 'idea creativity'.

The first essential step is to make a clear distinction between artistic creativity and idea creativity. The two are totally distinct even though they may overlap at some points. This is why I invented the term 'lateral thinking' to describe the creativity of ideas and thinking.

There are three ways of describing or defining lateral thinking. 'The thinking concerned with changing perceptions, concepts and ideas.'

'You cannot dig a hole in a different place by digging the same hole deeper.'

'In a self-organizing information system, asymmetric patterns are formed. Lateral thinking involves moving across patterns.'

We can now explore the basis and nature of lateral thinking and even design thinking tools to make it happen.

There is no mystery at all about idea creativity.

Idea creativity can be produced deliberately by

using methods based on the behaviour of a self-organizing information system that makes asymmetric patterns.

There is a close system relationship between humour and lateral thinking.

It is not surprising that we have failed to understand creativity. The philosophical approach of analysis will not help. The descriptive approach of psychology will not help. What is needed is an understanding of the basic system behaviour of the brain. Once this is understood, then creativity is easily explained.

There are three men, each of whom is holding a piece of wood. Each one drops the piece of wood.

In the first case the piece of wood falls downward.

In the second case the piece of wood moves upward.

In the third case the piece of wood stays where it was released.

This different behaviour is impossible to understand until we decide to look at the 'universe' of each person.

The first man is standing on the surface of the earth, so the wood falls downward.

The second man is standing under water, so the wood moves upward – since it floats.

The third man is in a spacecraft orbiting the earth with zero gravity, so the wood just stays where it was released.

If we tried to explain the behaviour of the second and third piece of wood in the universe of the first it would never make sense.

In a similar way, if we try to explain creativity in a 'passive' information system, we do not get anywhere.

We need to consider a 'self-organizing' information system. Such systems make patterns – as mentioned earlier in this book and in my book *The Mechanism of Mind* (Simon & Schuster 1969, Jonathan Cape and Penguin UK).

What happens if the pattern has a side track? Would we have to stop at every junction to decide which route to take? If we had to do so, life would be impossibly slow. This is not necessary. The way the nerves are linked up in the brain the dominant area of activity suppresses other areas. So we continue down the main track and side tracks are temporarily suppressed.

If, however, we enter the system along the side track then we can follow this back to the starting point – as shown in the diagram below. This gives rise to an asymmetric system. The route from A to B is not the same as the route from B to A.

FIGURE 2

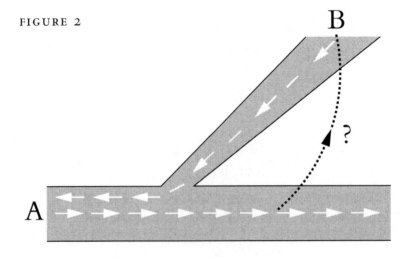

This asymmetric system is the basis of humour. Once the punch line is given then the 'logical' route back to the starting point is obvious.

An old man of ninety dies and goes down to hell. As he wanders around he sees a friend of his of around the same age. This friend has a beautiful young woman sitting on his knee. He asks:

'Are you sure this is hell, you seem to be having a good time?'

His friend replies:

'It is hell alright. I am the punishment for her.'

Creativity follows exactly the same mechanism. Our sequence of experience sets up the main tracks – for which we should be very grateful. The side tracks are suppressed as we efficiently use the main tracks or patterns.

If 'somehow' we enter through a side track then that track becomes obvious. This is the basis of idea creativity.

● ● ●

The purpose of lateral thinking is to provide that 'somehow' which takes us across (laterally) to the side track. These methods then become the formal tools of lateral thinking.

There are several lateral thinking tools. I shall describe just two here because they illustrate how necessary it is to understand the basic system behaviour of the brain.

The 'random input' method is most often used with a 'random word'. There is the subject about which you want some new ideas. You drop in a word, usually a noun, and you use this word to generate new ideas.

Now at this point any logician would get very upset. If the word is truly random then any random word would work for any subject. This would be a complete definition of nonsense.

Yet, in spite of the logician's objections, it works very powerfully in real life. It was this method that Carol Ferguson used with her workshops to generate twenty-one thousand ideas one afternoon.

The explanation is surprisingly simple.

A person living in a small town always takes the same main road when leaving his house. This road satisfies all travel needs. One day on the outskirts of the town his car breaks down and he has to walk home. He asks around for the quickest way back to his house. He follows the instructions and finds himself travelling home along a road he had never used before. In future he can use this new road.

In a patterning system, if you start at the periphery you can open up a route that you could never have opened up from the centre where the usual pattern dominance has been established.

The 'random word' because it is truly random is not part of any established pattern relating to the subject and so can open up a new route. It does occasionally happen that there is an obvious connection between the random word and the subject. In such cases you pick another word.

There is no mystery or magic about this at all. The simplicity of the method and its apparent illogical nature illustrate why the development of thinking depends on an understanding of the underlying information system. Playing with words will never be enough.

We can now consider another approach. This method is 'provocation'.

With provocation there may not be a reason for saying something until after it has been said.

With logic every step has to be correct, whereas with provocation proof is determined in hindsight – once you have got there.

There was a language need for the new word 'po'.

Language is about truth and an accurate description of the world around.

We are allowed to speculate about unknown possibilities. We can use words like: 'maybe'; 'suppose'; 'what if?'

Because language is about truth we are not permitted to say something which we definitely know to be wrong, rubbish, impossible or contradictory.

In creativity, because of the way the brain works, we have a need for provocation. Provocation is essential in any self-organizing system in order to move from a local equilibrium to a more global one.

As a result it was necessary to invent a new 'operating' word to allow us to use provocation. This new word is 'po' and it is described in several of my books. It is pronounced to rhyme with 'no'. It can be taken to indicate 'possibility', 'hypothesis', 'poetry', etc. All of these go beyond the known.

Here is a provocation.

'Po motor cars should have square wheels.'

Any engineer would be extremely upset at this suggestion because it contradicts so many principles.

...you would need a huge amount of energy
...the car would shake to pieces

...the ride would be extremely bumpy

...the wheels would collapse, etc.

All such comments are absolutely valid.

They are valid if we use our traditional thinking operation of 'judgement'. Judgement would indicate that 'square wheels' are an impossibility and that the idea is silly, ridiculous and without any merit at all.

Judgement demands that we compare what is offered with what we know to be 'true' and then reject what does not match. Judgement is part of 'rock logic' which is the logic of identity: this is so; this is not so; this fits; this does not fit.

Then there is 'water logic', which we have never developed. 'Water logic' is the logic of 'flow': what does this lead to; what happens next; where do we go from here?

Just as judgement is the operating tool of traditional logic so we need a new operating tool for 'water logic'.

This new operation is 'movement'. With movement we do not stop to consider whether something is right or wrong, we 'move' forward: what does this lead to?

So we apply 'movement' to the provocation about square wheels on motor cars.

As the wheel rotates the car would rise and fall. This is entirely predictable so the suspension could change accordingly to give a smooth ride.

From this comes the idea of 'adjustable suspension'. From this comes the idea of a vehicle for travelling over rough ground. The car itself would remain stable and the wheels would adjust to the bumpiness of the ground. The idea has been tried and does work.

'Po you die before you die'.

Once again this sounds illogical. How can you die before you die? Normal thinking and normal judgement would throw out the idea.

But Ron Barbaro, when he was president of Prudential Insurance (Canada), 'moved' forward from the provocation to develop 'living needs benefits'.

Life insurance normally pays up when you die. Living needs benefits means that a part of the money due could be paid if you got a serious illness so that you had funds to pay for extra medical care. This concept is now in use with many major insurance groups in North America. Ron Barbaro became president of Prudential Insurance (USA).

Ron Barbaro was a very good user of my work and even had the 'Six Hats' woven into the carpets at the Canadian headquarters.

'Po the factory should be downstream of itself.'

Again this is nonsense. How can the factory be in two places at once?

A factory placed on a river puts out pollution. Those downstream suffer from the pollution. The provocation follows.

From the provocation comes a very simple idea. If you build a factory on a river your input must be downstream of your own output. So you are the first to get your own dirty water. You now take more care to clean your effluent. I am told that this has now become legislation in several countries.

There are formal ways of setting up provocations (escape, reversal, distortion, etc.). There are formal ways of getting 'movement' (concepts, difference, circumstance, etc.). All these are described in detail in other books (such as *Serious Creativity* Harper Collins 1995) and training programmes.

● ● ●

My point in mentioning these two tools of lateral thinking here is twofold. The first intention is to show that idea creativity can arise from formal thinking but thinking that is different from traditional thinking. The second intention is to show that the design of new thinking tools demands an understanding of the broad information behaviour of the brain and that traditional description and analysis simply cannot do this.

Our traditional approach to creativity is remarkably feeble.

Imagine a person walking along a road. We stop the person and tie them with a rope. A violin is now produced. Obviously, the person tied up with the rope cannot play the violin.

So we say: 'This person cannot play the violin because he or she is tied up with the rope. If we cut the rope the person will be able to play the violin.'

Clearly, this is total nonsense. But that is how we have treated creativity for the last fifty years.

If you are inhibited you cannot be creative. This is true. If you are tied up with a rope you cannot play the violin.

So if we make you uninhibited you will be creative. This is not true: if we cut the rope that does not make you a violinist.

Approaches like brainstorming are well intentioned but very feeble. Their value lies not in the ability to generate ideas but in the motivation to seek to develop ideas that are suggested. The formal, structured methods of lateral thinking are much more powerful and productive.

Idea creativity is not a mystery. It is thinking in a self-organizing information system that makes asymmetric patterns.

Every valuable creative idea will always be logical in hindsight.

This is why we have never paid serious attention to creativity.

There is a singles tennis tournament. A player plays another player and the loser is eliminated. It rains much of the first week and the organizer has to cram the matches into the second week.

There are one hundred and thirty-one entrants. Clearly there is one final, two semi-finals, four quarter-finals, etc. There might be byes in the first round. How many matches are needed?

You can give this problem to a group of one hundred highly intelligent people and at most two of them will work it out in five seconds.

If there are one hundred and thirty-one players there will be one hundred and thirty losers. How is a loser produced? By a 'loser-producing match'. Are there any other sorts of matches? No. So the figure is one hundred and thirty matches.

This is totally logical in hindsight. So why do ninety-eight per cent of people not see it?

Every valued creative idea will always be logical in hindsight. This is almost by definition. If you can see the 'value' of the idea, you can create a logical pathway to that value.

History is full of examples of great discoveries which were made by chance, accident, mistake, anomaly, etc. but are then written up with an immaculate step-by-step, logical discovery process.

Imagine a crawling insect on the trunk of a tree. What are the chances of that insect getting to one specified leaf. At each branch point the chances diminish by one over the number of branches. In the average tree the chances may be no better than one in eight thousand. Now imagine the insect on a leaf. What are the chances of that insect getting to the trunk of the tree? The chances are one in one. There are no forward branches on the way down.

In any asymmetric system the route from A to B is not the same as the route from B to A.

Once again, it is failure to understand the nature of asymmetric (self-organizing) systems that has blocked our development of creativity.

We have maintained that if a creative idea is logical in hindsight, then proper logic should have got there in the first place. This is total nonsense in an asymmetric system.

It is this sort of nonsense which has prevented us from understanding creativity, from developing creativity and even from paying sufficient attention to creativity. That is one of the reasons the human race has never really learned to think. We set off along a track which was useful at first but is now restricting.

We are obsessed with problem solving.

We esteem critical thinking far too highly.

We are very much better at pointing out what seems wrong than at suggesting what might be better.

I have worked with many major corporations around the world. In many cases, not all, the basic strategy seems to be:

'Maintenance and problem solving.'

In practice this means keep things going as they are, from day to day. When problems arise then you solve these problems.

To this may be added the occasional 'me-too'. This means that if a competitor has come up with a new idea that seems successful, then you enter that area with your own version of the idea.

Now and then your investment banker may suggest a merger or an acquisition.

It is hardly surprising that business works this way because that is how the rest of society works. Keep things going and solve problems as they arise. There is no need to think about matters that are not problems: 'If it is not broken do not fix it.'

Here we see one of the less obvious dangers of the fundamental idiom of 'truth'. If something is 'true' then there is no point in thinking further about the matter. You cannot be more true than true. It is a small step from 'true' to 'right'. If this is 'right' there is no point in thinking further about it.

If something is 'not right' then that is a problem and we think about how to fix it.

The result is that there is a huge number of concepts, methods and processes which are far from the best and which could be greatly improved by thinking. These subjects never get any thinking because they are not perceived as 'problems'.

For example, the concept of 'democracy' could be greatly improved.

In 1971 I did some work for Shell Oil in London. In the course of the workshop I observed that oil wells were always drilled vertically downwards. I suggested that wells should go downward until they reached the oil-bearing stratum and then horizontally along the stratum.

Today, almost every oil well in the world is drilled in this 'horizontal' fashion.

The reason is that you get between three and six times as much oil from such wells as from the traditional wells.

I doubt whether my suggestion was actually instrumental in changing the drilling habits. The story illustrates how there are many things which are 'adequate' and which we do not think about but which could be greatly improved by some thinking attention.

The rim of a wine glass is round. This is because glasses used to be made by blowing a bubble of glass – and some are still made that way. There might also be a comparison with clay vessels which are made on a wheel and are also round.

I once suggested a new shape for a wine glass. Looked at from above, the top of a wine glass should be kite shaped. If you were thirsty you drank out of the broad area. If, however, you just wanted to sip and taste the wine you drank from the narrow area. I had some of these made up in Murano, Venice. There was a huge difference in the amount people drank depending on which area they chose.

Wine glasses have been roughly the same shape for three thousand years. Why could this change not have been made before? Perhaps no one perceived any value in drinking less because there were no drink-drive laws.

We are so complacent about the stability and general satisfactory state of society that we prefer to think only about problems. We expect that all matters will improve in small evolutionary steps without any special thinking – and without upsetting anyone.

As part of this stability and complacency we put a very high emphasis on 'critical thinking'. The word 'critical' comes from the Greek word for judge, 'kritikos'.

Amazingly, our academic establishments, at all levels, regard critical thinking as the highest form of thinking.

It is easy to see the protective value of critical thinking. It is a good protection against wild and crazy ideas and those who would disturb society with mystic flights of fancy.

If you are building a bridge or suggesting a new welfare programme it is useful to have someone cast a critical eye at your thinking.

In politics the role of critical thinking has reached a point where most people consider it to be absurd. Everything the other party proposes is nonsense – and the other way around. This is not really credible and people would like to see a more constructive and balanced approach.

We also tend to forget how very easy critical thinking can be.

If ninety-five per cent of an idea is valid but five per cent is more doubtful, we focus on that five per cent. If we did so in order to improve the idea by attention to that weak five per cent, then that would be valuable. We do not do this. We focus on the five per cent to suggest that if this five per cent is weak then the whole idea is worthless.

It is like condemning a grand new building because the door handles are not to your taste.

One of the main problems of critical thinking is its attraction for mediocre minds who are unable to be constructive or creative. If someone designs a simple chair, then that chair can be criticized as stark and boring. The chair may be compared to a prison chair or a hospital chair. It may be condemned as without style or character.

If the person had designed a more elaborate chair then that chair could be criticized as vulgar and fussy.

All the critic needs to do is to choose a position different from that which is offered and then to attack what is offered as differing from the critic's chosen position. This is hardly great thinking.

This is even worse if the critic obviously does not understand what he or she is criticizing. It is quite easy to make a good show of profound criticism without understanding the matter at all. Newspaper critics do this all the time – and even get chosen as 'Critic of the Year' as a result.

In most of the dialogues in which Socrates was involved (and as written up by Plato) there is no positive outcome at all. Socrates simply points out that something is wrong.

When the irritated listeners asked Socrates what was right, if everything was wrong, he declared that that was not his business. His business was to point out what was wrong.

We are back to the 'front left wheel of a car' analogy. Critical thinking is very valuable and has a necessary part to play in society. It is not, however, the most important aspect of thinking.

The most important aspect is constructive and creative thinking. You cannot design a better way forward just through judgement.

At one time language was the biggest help to human progress: for thinking, for communicating and for recording.

Today, language is by far the biggest barrier to human progress.

Language is an encyclopaedia of ignorance that forces us to look at the world in an old-fashioned way.

Let me make it clear that by 'language' I mean our existing languages, not the concept of a communicating system.

I also want to make it clear that I am not referring to the hundreds of different languages in the world today, although this variety may indeed restrict human progress (four hundred and twenty-eight languages in Papua New Guinea alone).

I am referring to ordinary language, whether it is English, French or Chinese.

I am conscious that these comments are likely to upset many people who are very happy with the richness, variety and utility of language. Such people may or may not choose to understand what I am writing about.

Words come into language at a relative stage of ignorance. They then become frozen into permanence.

These words then affect our thinking. They affect our communication. Worst of all, they affect our perception and force us to look at the world in a very old-fashioned way.

The word 'profit' is a simple example. In the early days of more exploitive capitalism, 'profit' came to mean 'excess profit' and 'exploitation'. The anti-capitalists and the Marxists emphasized this aspect. Today, profit needs to be seen as a normal part of the business process: for re-investment and to attract investors, etc.

One of the big dangers of language is that things which seem similar are lumped together. The existence of one word makes unnecessary the creation of other words.

This is the case with words like 'creativity' and 'design'. In an earlier part of the book I indicated the need to separate between artistic creativity and idea creativity. This is a real need and was the basis for the creation of the word 'lateral thinking'.

The word 'design' is hugely important. It is every bit as important as analysis but has been almost entirely neglected. Design is putting things together to deliver value. What could be more important?

Because 'design' is seen as dress design, graphic design, architectural design, the pure concept of design does not get any attention and is almost never taught as such.

The words 'failure' and 'mistake' have real meanings. If you set out to climb Mount Everest and do not get to the top that can be called a 'failure'. If a train driver mistakes a signal and causes a crash, that is a 'mistake'. If a nurse in hospital gives the wrong dose of a drug and kills the patient, that is a mistake.

If a business executive tries a new venture which for unforeseen reasons does not succeed, that is seen as a 'mistake' or 'failure'. That failure will affect the future career path of the executive. As a result executives are unwilling to try new things.

Yet there is a huge difference between a real mistake or a real failure and a 'fully justified venture which did not succeed for unforeseeable reasons'. Indeed that executive would have made a mistake if he or she had not undertaken the venture. We badly need a word for such activity.

We badly need a word for 'the way we look at something at this moment'. The word 'perception' is too broad.

We need a word for what I have called 'the logic bubble' in one of my books. This is that 'bubble' of experience, information, values and perception within which everyone acts perfectly logically. At least logically for that person but not for those who do not understand the 'logic bubble'.

When there is a concrete object like a 'computer' or a 'mobile phone' we are not bad at inventing new words. Apart from such new objects it is very difficult to get words into use. Furthermore they run the risk of being classified as 'jargon' by those who do not understand what is happening.

Language preserves the world we know but does not design the world we need to know.

It can be argued that the skilled use of language can describe any situation. This may indeed be so but the process is clumsy and not easy to repeat. It is inevitable that we shall need to move to a higher order language, a sort of coding for complex situations.

We might need a code which indicated:

'You are a good friend and I like you very much – but I would not want to be involved in business with you.'

I once read that the Eskimos had a similar expression which went: 'I like you very much but I would not want to go seal hunting with you.'

I have since been told that this may not be true, but as an illustration it stands.

Language is, of course, the crystallization of the recognition/ judgement/box system described earlier in the book. You have a word for friend and a word for enemy but no word for someone who can be both.

Language also suffers from the 'peak problem'. Some is good, more is better, more is not so good, yet more is worse, yet more is very bad. Freedom is good for children. Too much freedom may be bad.

Discipline is good but too much discipline is bad. Once the value (good or bad) has been attached to the language box then it is very hard to tell at what point the value begins to reverse. This leads to difficulty in argument, decisions and communication. We seek to overcome this problem with adjectives like 'harsh discipline' or 'irresponsible freedom' but the effect is far from satisfactory.

Our thinking is conditioned and trapped by language which by its very nature has more to do with the past than the future. We use silly blanket words like freedom, democracy and social justice to justify any behaviour to which we can attach these words.

We need simple ways of dealing with complexity rather than complex ways of dealing with simplicity.

Evolution fits the needs of the past not the needs of the future.

Evolution can optimize on the present and the past but not on the future. For that you need design.

Language has evolved over time to fit the changing needs of the moment. There is no element in language that prepares it to meet the needs of the future.

A man had a stroke. It was a small stroke. It was a most unusual stroke. There was only one small mental defect as a result of this stroke. He could not remember the names of vegetables. That is all. Everything else was unaltered.

The implications of this tiny defect are huge. Somewhere in the brain the names of vegetables are specifically recorded.

Why do we need names for vegetables?
There are those things that are red, shiny and round. They fit easily into the hand. There is a firm outer layer under the skin but the inside is more fluid with seeds.

It is a bit easier to say 'tomato'.

It is cylindrical with rounded ends. It may curve somewhat. The skin is deep green but the flesh inside is white. It is used sliced up in salads and the Greeks mix it with yoghurt.

It is simpler to say 'cucumber'.

We use names to capture in a simple and usable way what could probably be described with other language in a much more complicated way.

It seems that once the name is there, then this name has a location in the brain. It is a 'place'. The complex description, even if accurate, has no location in the brain. It is not a 'place' but an 'itinerary' or 'temporary journey'.

We do this for vegetables, but do we do this for human situations? There are words like 'surrender', 'bully', 'compromise', 'negotiate', etc. These do describe in a single word situations that are somewhat complex. There are, however, more complex situations which never get a word of their own.

A teenager has got herself into trouble. She needs help from her parents but she does not want the usual sermon and 'you should have listened to me' tirade. Does she say all this? Or, does she go to 'de Bono Code B' and say: 'Mum, I have an 8/1'.

In time Mum gets to know what 8/1 means. The first time she may have to look it up in the code book. It means: 'I am in trouble and I really need your help but I do not want the usual sermon, etc.' Both parties know exactly where they stand.

In a negotiation one party may say to another: 'I feel we have a code 15/6 here.' This means: 'We keep going over the same things again and again. Until the benefits are considerably increased I cannot agree with the deal.'

The de Bono Code Book (Penguin 2001) lays out a number of codes for travel, negotiating, project management, starting relationships, ending relationships, etc. Code B consists of arbitrary assigned numbers.

The codes become international. You can think into them in English and think out of them, simultaneously, in Japanese, German, Hindu, Russian, etc. They form an 'inter-language'. The main value is to clarify a complex situation just as the name of a vegetable clarifies a more complex description.

A few of the most commonly used codes will be remembered just as most people remember some telephone numbers. Other codes may be looked up in the code book or via a mobile phone reference service.

In addition to every other value, the codes enable someone to say something that might otherwise be embarrassing or awkward.

At Miami airport you sometimes hear: 'Code 13, code 20'. This is asking the person who is code 13 to carry out the operation which is code 20. The coding system means that the public address facility is not tied up with long operational requests. If a limousine picks you up at Los Angeles airport, the driver will radio back to headquarters: 'Code 9'. This means: 'I have picked up the passenger successfully and we are on the way to the destination.'

Television shows how New York police cars use codes all the time. This is to shorten communication time, to reduce ambiguity and to overcome poor radio reception in certain areas. So, 'code 37 at 24th and Lexington' might mean 'domestic violence situation and one party is armed.'

The main objection to codes might be as follows:

'They are unnecessary because ordinary language can do everything.' I have sought to point out that 'doing everything' is not the same as a code with its own brain location.

Another objection is that the numbered codes are ugly. This is true at first. The paintings of the Impressionists were ugly to those who wanted more Ingres and David.

'The codes would not be subtle enough.' You could make the codes as subtle as you liked. You could also write poetry with the codes: this is somewhere between this code and that; this is the code but there are tinges of this and that, etc. Shakespeare was such a professional that he would have welcomed codes. Juliet talking to Romeo from the balcony would have used a code to express her complex emotions: 'I love you dearly but we do not seem to be getting anywhere. Perhaps we had better call it a day.' This is a code 13/1. Romeo might reply with a code 13/3, which means: 'I am happy with the relationship. Things are going well. I thank you.'

The most important objection would be lack of uniformity in knowing the codes. You could not use the codes if the other party did not know them.

The more used codes could become universally known. You could carry a small card with a few codes on it. With mobile phones, computers, e-mail, etc. codes could be instantly accessed.

Something of the sort is inevitable. We do need to move to a higher order language to clarify complex situations instead of spending all our time trying to establish where we are at.

In addition to the value of fixed codes where numbers are assigned in an arbitrary manner, there is a need for a constructed code.

In the constructed code, a few fundamental concepts can be assembled in different ways to convey complex meanings. You only have to remember the nine fundamental concepts.

The de Bono Code Book (Penguin 2001) contains two codes. Code B is the arbitrary coding of a number of situations in different need areas. Code A is the constructed code.

In the constructed code, the sender puts together a meaning by using any combination of nine fundamental concepts, each of which is assigned a number.

The numbers can be arranged on a grid as shown in the book.

The meaning of the numbers is as follows:

7...This indicates 'presence'. The number indicates that the subject exists and is present and known.
8...This means 'system positive'. This is the general 'positive' indicator.

3...This is 'the people factor'. It could mean people in general, or specified people. In simple combinations it can mean I, we, you, they, etc.

1...This is the 'input factor'. This can mean 'what we start with' or, 'the present state of affairs'. A boiled egg starts with a raw egg.
2...This is the 'change factor'. This is a key concept and covers:

cause, change, effect, make happen, influence, etc. When something passes through the change process it is different when it comes out the other end.

6…This is the 'output factor'. This may represent the output we get. It may also represent the output we want to get – the objective. In general, it represents the 'result'.

5…This is the 'absence factor'. Something is not present. It is used in asking questions. You indicate what is absent and ask for it to be made present. It can also be used to ask for something 'to be removed'. A problem may need 'removing'.

4…This is the 'system negative' factor. It is the opposite of '8' as the system positive factor. It is the general negative indicator.

9…This is the 'time factor'. In combination it can mean present, past, future, etc. You can ask for something 'to be speeded up' and you can ask when a project will be completed, etc.

The numbers have been chosen to fit cultural sensitivities. In particular this applies to China, which will be a major user of the codes. There is great number sensitivity, particularly in Cantonese.

Full examples of the use of the constructed code (Code A) are given in *The de Bono Code Book* (Penguin 2001).

The two codes can be distinguished in use by a prefix, such as 00 before Code A.

I have mentioned the codes here not to describe them but to indicate the sort of powerful changes that may need to take place if we are to make significant progress. Being bogged down in the complacency of comfort of where we are, and vigorously defending that complacency, may not be the best way to move forward.

You can be very happy with horse- drawn vehicles but this does not design motor cars.

Why has it been so difficult for the human race to really learn how to think?

What are the existing barriers in society that make it very difficult to improve our thinking?

Why are we so content with a rather poor thinking system?

There are many ways of expressing roughly the same thing:

'If it is not broken don't fix it.'

'The adequate is the enemy of the best.'

We have a tolerably good thinking system and we cannot conceive of any better one. Our recognition/ judgement/box system seems to have served us very well in science and technology. That it has obviously not served us so well in human affairs we put down to human nature, emotions, etc. rather than a deficiency in our thinking.

We also have a system that is remarkably good at defending itself through defining the idiom in which it can be attacked.

We have a system that insists you must prove it 'wrong' before any change can be suggested. As the system is not at all wrong then no change is needed. It is very difficult, within the existing system, to say that our current thinking is excellent but inadequate; it is good for analyzing the past but not for designing the future.

Self-satisfaction, comfort and complacency are very difficult to budge.

Evolution produces a species that is highly adapted to one environment but not very efficient in a new environment.

Our thinking evolved to satisfy the needs of churchmen in the middle ages and then continued to evolve to defend a stable society. It was never intended to deal with a rapidly changing world which needs design as much as judgement.

● ● ●

Our education systems are mediaeval in their attitudes. Two of the most important subjects of all, value creation and thinking, are not taught.

In the United Kingdom youngsters leave school knowing the names of some of Henry VIII's wives and the date of the treaty of Utrecht. No doubt these are very important. The same youngsters have no idea how the corner shop works. Youngsters are never taught directly and explicitly how value is created in society: by politics, by business, by the police, by voluntary organizations, etc. Yet when they leave school they will be directly involved in value creation for themselves (even as entrepreneurs) and for society.

In the European Union twenty-five per cent of school time is spent on mathematics. Most people use no more than three per cent of the mathematics they learn at school.

There are three arguments for all the time spent on mathematics.

The first argument is that it is there, so we might as well teach it.

The second argument is that a youngster may want to become a rocket scientist so a good basis in mathematics is needed. We might as well teach singing in case a youngster wanted to become an opera singer. The mathematics needed for rocket science can be taught as part of that specialization course.

The mathematics requirements for entry into many university faculties is totally unrealistic and drives many youngsters to softer subjects that require no mathematics, such as law, media studies, etc. You need statistics in psychology even though you no longer work statistics out by hand – you plug them into a computer.

The third argument is that the discipline of mathematics trains 'the mind'. This may or may not be so. But if this is indeed the intention then there are other, more powerful, ways of training the mind which go beyond the 'game' of mathematics. If ninety per cent of the errors in thinking are errors of perception then we should spend a great deal more time teaching perception.

This leads on to the second subject that is not taught. This is the most fundamental subject of all: thinking. Nothing is more important to an individual than the ability to think. Thinking changes emotions. Thinking changes behaviour. Thinking can increase self-esteem and self-confidence: you can cope with the world instead of drifting like a cork in a stream.

Some schools are now beginning to teach thinking directly as a subject. Some schools teach 'critical thinking' which is valuable but old-fashioned and totally insufficient. What is needed is practical skill in thinking – not just reflection on what happens during thinking. Venezuela is one of the very small number of countries where the teaching of thinking is now mandatory in the curriculum. Europe is rather far behind. China may well move ahead of Europe and the USA in this respect.

Then there are the universities with their emphasis on scholarship, history and the past.

In any town there are restaurants which come and go with a rapid turnover according to demand and need. Is there an equivalent turnover of university faculties with new ones coming in and old ones moving out?

Why does no university in the world have a faculty of 'thinking' or a chair of thinking?* Because it is not important. Because it cannot be done. Because it is already done under another heading.

Here we come to 'philosophy'. At the beginning philosophy tried to look at thinking but soon ended up creating 'the game of logic'. This is immensely valuable but, as I have emphasized throughout this book, it is only one aspect of practical thinking. In fact logic is far less important than perception in everyday thinking.

Then philosophy gradually got involved in the analysis of

---

* Since the writing of this book, the University of Pretoria have made me
'Professor of Thinking'. In addition the University of Advancing
Technology in Arizona has made me Da Vinci Professor of Thinking.
Dublin City University has made me Professor of Constructive Thinking.

meaning, the analysis of concepts and word games in general. The practical utility of these has not always been very evident. I doubt whether the teaching of philosophy (or some aspect of it) to unemployed youngsters for five hours would increase their employment rate five fold (as did the teaching of thinking).

This is not to devalue philosophy, which has its role and value in society, but to emphasize that there is a big difference between philosophy and the practical teaching of thinking as a skill. Making youngsters aware of mistakes is only a very small part of thinking.

Psychology is not involved in the development of direct thinking skills. The descriptive aspects of psychology are quite different from the design aspects needed. Psychology is about describing what happens – not about making it happen.

In general, universities have a sort of stranglehold on education in society. They also have a stranglehold on thinking since all matters in this area are, sooner or later, referred to universities for their judgement.

It is the nature of these 'locked in' systems that makes human progress so very slow.

The press may be the only area in society where criminality is approved, sanctioned and even endorsed.

Blame it on democracy as no politician dare upset the press.

Blame it on democracy as the need for a free press relieves the press of any need to be responsible.

In the United Kingdom, a poll showed that fifty-six per cent of youngsters did not trust the press.

This should be an alarming statistic. For older people with much more experience of the behaviour of the press, to show some distrust might be understandable. But for youngsters, with their readiness to accept things on authority, the figure is truly shocking.

The press thinks of itself as representing 'truth' and 'honesty' in society. Most people no longer see it that way.

The British press is regarded by many as the most dishonest in the world. I have been told this by people from many different countries.
This is not to imply that all the British press is dishonest, for it is only a small part that is dishonest. Surprisingly, however, the British press takes a sort of defiant pride in its dishonesty.

Some time ago a young journalist wrote up an interview with me in the Guardian newspaper. Many people regarded that interview as rather dishonest. My tape recording of the interview suggested that certain things attributed to me had not actually been said by me. For further details on this visit www.mediadishonesty.com.

Now that sort of interview is common enough. What is rather more bizarre is that the journalist in question was made Young Journalist of the Year partly on the basis of that interview. This was a British Press Award, which presumably represents the press as a whole.

I have to admit that what sometimes seems at first sight to be dishonesty is actually sheer stupidity. Another British Press Award went to the Critic of the Year. This person then wrote a review of a book which at first sight seemed dishonest but was more reasonably explained by the critic not having the faintest idea about what he was writing. Dishonesty is culpable but stupidity is only regrettable.

In matters such as these it is necessary to write from personal experience.
Important as these deficiencies and dishonesties of the press may be, there is a far more serious matter.

Other than in day-to-day conversation or in the thinking connected with their work, the only thinking most people are exposed to is what they read in the press. The press has the opportunity to make a wonderful contribution to society by encouraging better thinking. Instead the reader gets little more than advocacy, crude polemics, sensationalism and very selective perception. Amongst the journalists there are some very good thinkers, but they do not seem able to exert much influence over the rest.

There seems to be less danger with other media such as radio, television, films, etc. In such media you get to experience people and their opinions directly, not through the selective perception and shaping of a journalist with a particular agenda. In my experience, radio is the most honest of all the media. This may be because radio has always sought to be honest. It is doubtful if press journalists ever did.

If we choose not to give a subject any importance then in the eyes of society that subject has no importance.

Individuals can still make their personal choice.

What society chooses to recognize becomes important in that society.

In Finland many of the statues in the streets and square are to architects. Finland has a world–class reputation in architecture.

In Paris, the statues are to thinkers and philosophers. French society prides itself on its philosophical fluency.

In London most of the statues are to warriors and generals because that was important for running the Empire.

In the United Kingdom, the recognition system is pathetically political. If you contribute money to the party in power you get rewarded. If you excel in football, cricket or pop music you will get your recognition because this will please the voters. The true test of merit is rather more severe. How many of those 'contributions to society' will endure past the next ten years?

It is said that countries get the governments they deserve. It could equally be said that countries only get the talents they are able to recognize.

In South Africa a group of university professors compiled a list of the two hundred and fifty people who had made the most significant contribution to humanity in the whole known history of the human race. I was told that I was on that list for my contribution to human thinking. I wonder how many sports stars or rock singers are on that list.

Many years ago the Minor Planets Naming Committee of the International Astronomical Union chose to name a small planet after me. This was at the request of the European Creativity Society who had asked their members who had most influenced them.

It seems that I am one of the fifty people chosen by the consultant company Accenture as being the most influential in business thinking.

Do such things matter very much? Not in themselves, but unless 'thinking' comes to be recognized as a key factor in human progress, we are not going to get much progress.

At the moment there are a growing number of people around the world who are beginning to realize the importance of improving human thinking – and this number will continue to grow.

In summary it may be said that our existing thinking system is excellent at analysis, judgement and recognition. The system seeks 'truth'.

We need to develop much better thinking for creativity and design. That thinking would seek 'value'.

You can analyze the past but you have to design the future.

I need to repeat here the analogy I have used so often in this book: the front left wheel of a motor car may be excellent but it is not enough by itself.

Our existing thinking system may be excellent – it certainly considers itself to be excellent – but it may not be good enough for further progress.

Judgement, recognition and truth are good at telling us 'what is'. They are no good at designing 'what can be'.

So the first point is that our existing thinking does not equip us to be creative. As a result we rely on chance creativity and chance creative individuals.

Because of this lack of creative skill we have to rely on gradual evolution to shape our ideas and our institutions. That is a slow and inefficient process.

We are unable to challenge existing concepts in order to develop better ones. You do not need to prove a concept to be wrong in order to create a better concept.

Because we are weak at creativity, we are also weak at design. Without design we are unable to use all the opportunities provided by technological, demographic and cultural change. Because we are weak at design we are unable to design new values and new ways of delivering value.

So there are important things which our existing thinking is simply not able to do.

Then there are the faults within our existing system. There is the problem with 'boxes' and 'categories' which leads to discrimination, persecution, war, etc. and also makes conflict resolution so very difficult.

There is the problem of language and its inadequacies. Language is an encyclopaedia of ignorance which forces us to perceive the world in a very old fashioned way.

There are strong needs for new words in language. There is also a need for a higher order language to describe complex situations. Our existing thinking puts a lot of emphasis on logic. Yet most of our thinking, and almost all the errors, take place in perception. We have done nothing at all about perception.

Then we have argument, which is a crude and primitive way of exploring a subject. It is mainly concerned with case making and proving the other party wrong. This can mean that if the other party is poor at arguing then you are 'right' because you win the argument. But you may not be right at all. 'Parallel thinking' is a much better way of exploring a subject.

A glass may be excellent for drinking wine but not so good for drinking hot tea.

How did our existing thinking system come about?

Primitive man probably had a keen recognition system: what was good and what was bad. This might then have been supplemented by a naming system so you could communicate to others where lurked danger and where food might be found. Communication was also needed for cooperative endeavours.

Now we jump to the ancient Greek thinkers who made so remarkable a contribution to human thinking. For example the very important concept of the 'hypothesis' which is key in science.

The Gang of Three made an astonishing contribution with the system of categories, recognition and the 'game of logic'. Those contributions have lasted until today and are in everyday use.

After the Dark Ages came the Renaissance and people were encouraged to use their own thinking rather than just accept dogma. Through the Arabs in Spain, Greek and Roman thinking was re-introduced into Europe.

At that time the Church was largely in charge of education, intellectual culture and thinking. Most of the smartest people worked with the Church. The Church had little need for creativity and design. But what was really important was 'truth' and the means to demonstrate this. The result was an emphasis on argument with which to prove heretics wrong.

Perception was not as important as logic because the 'starting concepts' were given in Church thinking. They were a matter of faith and not experience. So perception got little attention.

Although over the centuries concepts and values changed, the fundamental method of thinking did not.

● ● ●

So what has changed today?

The fundamental change is that for the first time in history we can move beyond words and descriptions to examine the behaviour of the information system of the brain itself. This means we can understand creativity and design creative tools. It means that we can understand patterning behaviour.

Another change, related to the first, is that we can understand perception (patterns) and the huge importance of perception. We are beginning to realize, that in practical terms perception is the most important part of thinking. So we can design tools to improve our perception.

Because we can begin to understand the importance of brain chemicals we can design processes like the parallel thinking of the Six Hats where the modes of thinking are separated out.

What has also changed is an increasing realization of the importance of 'design'. We need to be able to design our way forward rather than just problem solve and let evolution provide progress.

As change occurs more rapidly we need the design process to make the best use of the change. Judgement is simply not enough. With judgement we can accept or reject but we cannot design ways of delivering value.

Finally, increasing experience with these new methods (CoRT, lateral thinking, parallel thinking) shows that they are both practical and powerful.

It is no longer a matter of just complaining about the inadequacies of traditional thinking. We can develop and use newer methods.

So?

So what?

So what needs to be done?

So what can be done?

So what will be done?

And...

1. There is a need to appreciate that thinking is the most fundamental human skill. The quality of our future will depend directly on the quality of our thinking. This needs proper recognition.

2. Thinking is a skill that can be taught, learned and improved. It is not just a matter of intelligence. There are many highly intelligent people who are poor thinkers, just as there are many less intelligent people who are good thinkers. The relationship between thinking and intelligence is like the relationship between the horse power of a car and the skill of the driver. You may have a powerful car driven badly and a less powerful car driven well.

3. Thinking skills can be taught across all ages, abilities, backgrounds and cultures. I have taught thinking to four year olds (in the Low's school in Singapore) and to ninety year olds (Roosevelt university). I have taught thinking to

Nobel Prize laureates and to Down's syndrome youngsters. I have taught thinking to senior executives. Colleagues, like Susan Mackie, have taught thinking to illiterate miners in South Africa. Other colleagues, like Norman Demajo, have taught thinking to prisoners with very positive results.

4. It is not a matter of discussing the philosophy of thinking or of analyzing the nature of thinking.

    There is a need to learn and practise simple practical thinking tools that can be used in everyday life. This gives youngsters increased confidence in their ability to deal with the world. It should also be demanded by democracy.

5. The new methods that I have developed have been thoroughly tried out in the real world. Nevertheless, they are only a beginning and much more will be done once we take 'thinking' seriously. There is the 'CoRT' programme that is widely used in schools throughout the world. This is for improving perception. There are the formal tools of lateral thinking which enable creativity to become a deliberate process.

    These are used in business in other organizations as well as in schools and universities. There is the Six Hats Method of parallel thinking which allows a much better exploration of a subject than traditional argument. This is becoming more widely used. There is the 'flowscape' method for mapping perceptions. There are the Six Action Shoes for defining different modes of action. There are the Six Value Medals which provide a framework for looking at value. Then there are the codes for clarifying complex situations. There is very much more that needs to be done.

6. There is a need to separate artistic creativity from idea creativity. The creativity involved in generating ideas is a

thinking skill that can be taught through the methods of lateral thinking. It should be taught as a necessary part of all thinking.

7. There is a need to realize that most of the mistakes of ordinary thinking are not mistakes of logic at all but mistakes of perception (the work of David Perkins). This is extremely important because teaching youngsters to avoid logical mistakes does not have much effect on perception.

8. Changes in perception will dramatically effect emotions and behaviour. The use of logic will not have these effects.

9. There is a fundamental need to realize that our traditional thinking methods based on analysis, judgement, recognition, boxes, categories and logic are excellent. They are excellent but insufficient.

10. There is a need to realize that the thinking involved in finding out 'what is' (truth) is not the same as the thinking involved in creating 'what can be' (value).

11. I would like to see 'thinking' as a mandatory subject in its own right on the curriculum of all schools in all countries. Unless an education system does this then that system wastes up to two thirds of the talent in that society. Those youngsters who are not good at the academic game leave school with nothing except the sense that they are stupid and cannot do anything. On the contrary, they may be excellent thinkers – if given the chance.

12. Critical thinking is an important part of thinking and has a role to play. But it is not enough just to teach critical thinking. Judgement does not have any constructive power.

13. I would like to see every university in the world having a faculty of 'thinking' and a chair of thinking. This should be very practical in nature – and separate from both philosophy and psychology.

14. 'Design' should have a much more central place in both schools and universities. Analysis, judgement and criticism are not enough for progress.

15. I would like to see constructive and creative intelligence rated above critical intelligence.

16. I would like to see the parallel thinking of the Six Hats method used in business discussions, in courts of law (for instance with juries) and even in parliament. There is a need to encourage this method in schools instead of keeping all the emphasis on 'debate'.

17. Before any negotiating conference there is a need for a 'design' conference. The purpose of the design conference is to create new alternatives, new possibilities, new concepts and new ways forward. When the 'negotiating' conference then follows, there is much more to work with. During negotiations it is very difficult to bring forth new ideas because they are immediately seen as judgement positions, in favour of the side putting forward the new idea. In the design conference ideas are simply put on the table with no commitment. There is an apparent need for just such a 'design conference' in the Middle East.

18. There is a real need for a World Centre for New Thinking to carry out those thinking functions which a representative body like the United Nations can never do. The Centre would generate new alternatives and possibilities and new concepts to help design the way forward. The Centre would

organise and facilitate 'new thinking conferences' on any issue. The Centre would help in conflict resolution. Such a Centre has now been set up in Malta in one of the ancient buildings left by the Knights of Malta.

19. At last and for the first time in history, we can move beyond descriptions and word games to see human thinking as the behaviour of the human brain. As a self-organizing information system the brain allows incoming information to organize itself as 'patterns'. These are immensely useful and allow us to exist in a complex world. The patterns also determine perception and selective perception. The patterns are 'asymmetric', which gives rise to the surprises of both humour and creativity.

20. All valued creative ideas will be 'logical' in hindsight. In an asymmetric system this does not mean that better logic would have obtained such ideas in the first place. There is a need to appreciate this.

21. There is an important role for history in society but there is an equally important role for 'design'. Universities, in general, spend far too much time on the 'scholarship' of history rather than the energy of design. The balance could be adjusted. We have to live in the future not in the past.

22. The media, and the press in particular, could play a far more constructive role in developing thinking skill in society. A constant diet of carping, criticism and occasional dishonesty may not be enough. It may not even be what readers want.

23. The International Conference on Thinking was started by an American teacher, William Maxwell, who was teaching my work in schools in Fiji. This conference has grown and

grown over the years and has become very successful. It is a measure of the neglect of the 'subject' of thinking that such a conference is so recent.

24. We need to be cautious about the use of 'truth' which can be used to justify almost anything. There are truths which are logically based on arbitrary perceptions, assumptions or beliefs. There are 'game truths' where you set up the game and ask people to accept the truths you find. There are 'circular truths' where you just circle back to your starting point — which was never itself proved.

25. We need to be cautious about language which may trap us into older perceptions that need changing. We should not be bullied by the apparent authority of language. There are many gaps where we badly need new words. At other times existing words capture things which are really different (creativity is an example).

26. There is a need to become aware of whole new thinking operations. For example, the operation of 'provocation' could never be permitted under our existing thinking system. Yet provocation is a mathematical necessity in any self-organizing system (like the brain). With provocation comes the new word 'po' to signal the operation. With provocation, comes the new mental operation of 'movement' where we look at an idea not in a judgement mode but with the intention of 'moving forward'.

27. I once wrote *Handbook for a Positive Revolution* (Penguin 1992) for Brazil. The idea was to get change through being constructive and active rather than just being against things. I am told that there is a country where every youngster entering school is given a copy of the book by the

government.

28. As chairman of the council for several years of Young Enterprise Europe, I saw how young people at school enjoyed setting themselves a task and then carrying it out. In this way they got a sense of achievement beyond the judgement of a teacher. The tasks they set themselves involved starting up and running a mini-business. It seems to me that this need for action and achievement is wider than business. So I am establishing a new organization called YEAH, which stands for Young Energy for Action and Help. This is a structure for youngsters to set up small teams. The teams then choose a task, which may be helping others or carrying out a project. They then 'think' how to do it and proceed to do it.

29. There is a real need for a higher order language to describe complex situations. The two codes I have suggested are a step in that direction. I am conscious how difficult the first stages of acceptance can be for something as radical as this. But it is a necessary direction for progress.

30. My brother Peter has been doing an excellent job teaching my work in places as diverse as Siberia, China, Argentina and the Dominican Republic. More and more countries are becoming aware of the power of simple thinking.

31. The Internet is becoming a very useful means for communication. The two sites most directly related to my work are www.edwarddebono.com and www.edwde bono.com.

32. Perhaps the most important point of all is to understand that self-organizing systems reach 'equilibrium points'. Any change away from these points seems negative at first – so we remain fixed at such points. We need to be ready to challenge the

comfort and complacency of such points. There are many concepts, processes and institutions in society that can be greatly improved – once we are prepared to challenge them. Our traditional habits of thinking are only one example.

33. I hope that at least some of the people reading this book will not react in a defensive manner. I hope that some of them will not rush to defend our traditional thinking habits and our language as perfect and beyond challenge. Those who do react in this defensive manner will get nothing from the book except another exercise in traditional thinking. In any case, I have made clear that our existing habits are excellent – but not enough.

34. It is important to point out that the methods suggested in this book do work very powerfully in the real world. It is no longer a matter of 'theorizing' whether or not they should work. They do work.

What is next?

What is new?

What different thinking system might there be? Could the human brain handle any thinking system other than the one we now have?

There are several levels of difficulty with anything new that is suggested.

Anything new is compared to what exists and the difference is usually seen as negative. The example of the Impressionist painters has been given before in this book.

Those who are sure of the 'perfection' of 'what is' see no need for something new.

Those whose expertise and authority are tied up in the existing system do not want to risk that by trying something new.

Then there is the awkwardness and clumsiness of the transition period of change. Once everyone has learned and got used to the new thing then the value of the new thing may be obvious. Until that point, however, the value is not obvious. This applies to the proposed codes.

● ● ●

One of the problems with our traditional box and judgement system is that something is either in the box or outside the box. If the item is in the box then it partakes of all the attributes that go with the box.

An example was given before of 'friend' and 'enemy'. What happens with someone who is mainly friend but capable of being an enemy? What happens to someone who is a rather 'weak' friend?
If, instead of boxes, we had two poles things would be different. One pole would be labelled 'friend' and the other would be labelled 'enemy'. A particular person might be placed half way between the poles, or two thirds of the way towards the enemy pole. This would make more sense, but could the brain, and language, cope with such a system?

After a particular film it became quite common to rate 'beauty' on a scale from one to ten. So a particular girl might be rated a nine or a seven. In the same way a person might be a nine on the friendship scale. Another person might be a seven – leaving you to wonder whether the missing three grades represented carelessness or 'enemy behaviour'.

From the two-pole system we might go to a several pole system which soon becomes a sort of 'field effect'. We might imagine a sort of contour map of a situation according to the different values involved. A computer could handle this – but could the human brain? Once the contour map had been drawn then we would flow, like water, along the best gradient which would become our path of action.

● ● ●

In art appreciation students are often asked not to look at the 'things' in a painting but to look at the space between things.

In our thinking we tend to look at 'things' and then look to see how they relate. We can imagine a type of thinking in which we looked at relationships and then at the things involved. This could mean focusing on 'values' not on things. Then we look around to see how the values might be delivered and this involves things. This begins to look very like the design process which is so important.

With thinking we have always been taught to look for specifics and to look for precision. This is not always the case. The very vagueness of a broad concept opens up far more than the specifics of a narrow idea. One of the secrets of good thinking is the ability to handle broad concepts.

When children are asked to design a process or a machine to do something, they put in a small panel with a button on it. Against the button is an explanation: 'If you press this button it all happens'. Here the broad concept is an escape from having to provide details. Broad concepts should be used as 'breeders' to breed narrower concepts which in turn breed a large number of specific ideas (this is the 'concept fan' method in lateral thinking).

• • •

There is a real need in language for a very vague word which means: 'the thing that is needed here'. A surgeon might say: 'We need "something" to get the edges of the skin to stick together'. This 'something' could then be: sutures, staples, glue, clips, etc.

The 'something' approach is usable but awkward. We would have to say, 'The something needed here has to be safe, cheap, sterile, removable, aesthetic, strong, etc.' We could have a single word, for example 'the requiron'. This means: 'that which is needed at this point'. We would then say: 'The requiron should be easy to apply and easy to remove; it should be strong but light; it should be sterile, etc.'

With the 'requiron' we describe the shape of a hole. Then we look around for things which would fit that hole. Just like those children's toys where the child has to fit the right shape into the hole.

'The requiron is that a few readers should see the value of this book and make my crusade for better thinking their crusade as well.'

'The requiron is that the tax payers should directly see the benefit of the extra tax. Another requiron is that a tax payer could direct the tax to an area of his or her choice. The general requiron is that the tax be transparently beneficial.'

At first the 'requiron' may seem awkward and unnecessary, since we can use words like 'need' and 'something'. In time, however, the value grows as you get used to using the new word.

● ● ●

In general, the power of the possibility system is under valued in thinking. We are aware of the huge importance of the hypothesis in science but even so are almost apologetic about it. Even the standard (Popper) approach is flawed. If you only look at the evidence through the most reasonable hypothesis, then you only get one perspective. You should at least have a second hypothesis, even if less reasonable.

We are quick to judge an opinion or a perception as 'right' or 'wrong'. We are not prepared to hold the opinion as a 'possible' and then to explore under what circumstances or with what values the opinion might make sense. The 'possible' holding box is much less used than the 'yes' or 'no' boxes.

The whole concept of provocation opens up the 'forward value' of a statement as opposed to the usual 'backward value'.

In general, the trend in thinking is going to be much more towards 'design' and 'value' than our existing habits, which are concerned with 'judgement' and 'truth'.

Nevertheless, there is a need to design thinking tools and habits that are simple and effective for 'people thinking'. Computers will be able to carry out very complex thinking, as they do with mathematics, but people will still need to think in a more constructive way than they do at the moment.

The coding system opens up fascinating new possibilities in terms of thinking and mental operations.

'Hodics' is the study of paths and patterns.

A challenge to the concept of cause and effect: because B follows A does not mean that A has caused B.

A new, and necessary, punctuation mark.

At the end of this section I shall be introducing a simple new punctuation mark to be added to our existing marks. This new mark covers a function that is not yet covered.

The word 'hodics' comes from the Greek word for road. Hodics is the study of paths, or patterns and of routes.

'If the next step has a higher probability in one direction rather than in any other direction, there may be a pattern.'

You are on a boat floating down the river. You pass town A on the riverbank. A little later you pass town B. This happens every time you go down that stretch of river. Town B happens to follow town A. There is no question of town A 'causing' town B.
You walk down the village high street towards the railway station. On your right you pass Henry, the butcher. Next comes Jones, the newsagent. A little further on there is the general store, and then the pharmacy. The sequence is always the same.

Every word in language only makes sense because each letter follows the preceding letter as it should. With the word 'cat' the 'a' follows the 'c'. Then the 't' follows the 'a'. The spelling should always be the same.

A chrysalis turns into a beautiful butterfly. An egg turns into a chicken. Youth turns into middle age. One thing follows another with an inevitability. A cup of hot tea grows cold.

All these processes have a similar 'following' characteristic. We can use different words to describe the process:

...A is followed by B

...A leads to B

...The sequence goes from A to B

...The pattern goes from A to B

...A changes into B

...B comes after A

There may be a certain expectation and a certain inevitability, but this does not mean that A has caused B. When sunshine follows a storm this does not mean that the storm has caused the sunshine.

'Cause and effect' might be seen as a special case of the more general concept of A leads to B. There are times, however, when we need to use the more general concept.

In the brain we have a mass of inter-connected neurons. Each neuron can become active and signal this activity to connected neurons which may be close by or at a distance. The activity is signalled down the 'nerves' themselves.

The nerves are like 'wires' in appearance and general function but very different in behaviour. A copper wire conducts electricity much as a pipe might conduct water. With nerves it is different. Imagine a series of hills and on the top of each hill there is a man with a pile of firewood and a box of matches. As soon as a person sees a fire lit on the nearby hill, he lights his own fire. The next person does the same. So the fire seems to travel from hill to hill. This was the method used both in England and in Malta to signal a sea borne attack. The important thing is that each point has its own energy which is 'triggered' by a signal.

Neurons are activated by signals from neurons with which they have been previously associated. An accumulation of signals can cause a neuron to 'fire' or become active. The neuron now contributes to the activation of other neurons.

If this were all that happened, then every time we opened our eyes we would get an epileptic fit.

This does not happen because there is a key 'inhibiting factor'. When neurons become active they contribute to the inhibition of other neurons.

The result is that only the group of inter-connected most sensitized neurons will be active. All others will be inhibited or suppressed.
If this were all, then activity would remain permanently with that group of neurons.

But the neurons run out of energy just as the hill-top signallers might run out of firewood. This is the extremely important 'tiring factor' which is so important in the brain and so despised by electronic engineers.

The tiring factor means that the original cluster of activated neurons gets 'tired' and stops its activities (it later recovers). The inhibition dies down.

Another cluster of neurons which has been ready to 'fire' but had been inhibited by the first cluster, now becomes active.

And so the process goes on. Activity moves from cluster A to cluster B and on to cluster C and perhaps back to cluster A. Each active area follows another active area in a typical pattern sense.

These patterns depend on past experience, present input, background chemicals, other brain patterns produced internally (thinking frameworks), etc.

The process is simply one of 'B follows A' or 'A leads to B' as described earlier in this section.

It is important to realize that A does not cause B. Nor is the energy conducted from A to B, as in electric wiring.

A boy shouts to another boy at a street corner. The second boy shouts to a third boy, etc. It is not the same shout that is being transmitted.

In the brain, it is not just clusters of neurons that matter but the whole 'neural state'. One state then leads to another state.
The word 'state' is a general term meaning 'things as they are'. A dining table at the beginning of a meal is in a different state from the state in the middle of the meal and from the state when the meal has been completed. 'State' includes all the elements and all the factors. The 'state of the economy' includes all the factors involved. The 'state of health' includes all the factors involved.

States change into other states. One state may lead to another. There may be a sequence of states.

Changes of state can indeed be expressed in ordinary written language by using words like 'leads to' or 'is followed by'.
The design of a specific punctuation device to cover this concept is not just to make simpler this 'A to B' concept as it now occurs. Such a value might be worthwhile. There is, however, a more

important value.

If we can make this 'flow' concept more readily available then people will find it easier to start 'thinking' this way. This is part of the 'water logic' thinking that has been mentioned earlier. The emphasis is less on 'what is?' than on 'where does this go?'

The punctuation device is the double forward slash, '//'. The double slash symbolizes a road or a path which might be represented by two parallel lines.

The double slash means: 'this leads to' or 'this is followed by'.

There is inflation and political instability in a country // people take money out of banks send it abroad, buy property or buy jewellery.

There is a growth in Internet romance sites // more attention to writing skills and poetry; more marriages outside national boundaries; a lot of disasters and disappointments.

The September 11 attack on New York had a powerful effect // more nationalism, more hedonism, less travel outside the USA.

In this use of the // the given state comes first and is then followed by the changed state. This use of the // is quite straightforward.

This state is followed // by this state.

There are further uses of the device when a question is being asked.
? // there are despondent and gloomy views among the youth of Australia about the future.

? // there is a rise in the number of unmarried mothers. In some countries this now exceeds fifty per cent.

? // there has been a steady fall in newspaper readership in the USA.

In such cases we are really asking: 'What has lead up to this present situation?' We might usually ask: 'What are the causes of this situation?' There might be a large number of factors none of which is a cause in itself but taken together there is a 'state' which leads on to the next state.

For example, with unmarried mothers there may be a combination of financial independence; hearing about friends who are single mothers; magazine articles; boorish behaviour of men; unhappy family backgrounds; feminism, etc. All together such factors create a state which leads in to the next state.
There is a further use of the double slash device. In this case we give the situation and then ask: 'What might this lead to?'

The mayor of London is proposing to charge cars a fee for entering the city centre //?

It is claimed that there is a lowering of examination standards //?

It is suggested that in a government election, those voters who are unsuccessful in their choice should pay ten per cent less tax, as compensation //?

In the last example it might be that voters would vote tactically for the party most likely to lose (which might then win). It would be interesting to see at what 'price level' voters would give up their political right to choose.

There are further minor uses. For example it might be asked, 'Does this really lead to that?' The element of doubt is a sort of question.

There might be a large shift in production to countries like China where wages are very much lower //? renewed pressure for protectionism.
This punctuation device is offered here for a number of reasons:

- to show that even something as firmly established as punctuation is not beyond improvement.

- to provide a convenient way of dealing with 'A leads to B' situations.

- to encourage people to think in terms of 'water logic' and the flow from one state to another.

Although the device is intended for punctuation in written thinking, it can also have an indirect effect on thinking itself. We can more easily think of one state leading on to another.

Because it is more important than any other human activity, 'thinking' needs far more attention and recognition than it currently gets. The neglect is astonishing.

Our traditional thinking methods are far from perfect. They have great deficiencies and some dangers. They are concerned with 'what is' rather than with 'what can be'.
There are simple new methods that work powerfully in action.

There is very much more to be done.

The human race needs to learn how to think.

Defensive complacency is dangerously stupid.

IOAM, AUGUST 23RD, 2002.
Chateau du Planty, France.

Epilogue

We need to do far more with our human thinking methods. We have been far too complacent with a system that is excellent in some regards but dangerously inadequate in others. The fact that this system is securely enshrined in our society makes any change difficult – but all the more necessary.

The new methods outlined in this book do make a huge difference in practice, but they are only a beginning. There is a great deal more to be done.

It may well be that in the future we will have 'mental contour maps' on computers which will guide and determine our thinking. The key question is whether our future thinking will need to be done by computers or whether there is room for improvement in human thinking done by human beings. I believe in both possibilities.

Computers will eventually be programmed to do powerful, multi-factorial thinking for us. At the same time, new concepts, new words and new methods will greatly extend the power of people thinking.

There is a long way to go. Why are we so very slow in getting going?

● ● ●

Selected books by Edward de Bono

The de Bono Code Book, Penguin, 2001

Handbook for a Positive Revolution, Penguin, 1992

I Am Right, You Are Wrong, Penguin, 1991

The Mechanism of Mind, Simon & Schuster, 1969, Penguin UK

Serious Creativity: Using the Power of Lateral Thinking to Create New Ideas, HarperCollins, 1995